R. H. Parker was born in North Walsham, Norfolk, in 1932. He read Economics at University College, London, from 1951 to 1954. He then served three years' articles in the City of London before becoming a member of the Institute of Chartered Accountants in England and Wales in 1958. Since then he has practised accounting and taught at universities and business schools in Australia, Britain, France and Nigeria. He is the author of *Management Accounting: An Historical Perspective* (1969), *Macmillan Dictionary of Accounting* (1984), *Papers on Accounting History* (1984) and *The Development of the Accountancy Profession in Britain to the Early Twentieth Century* (1986); he is joint author of *Topics in Business Finance and Accounting* (1964), *Accounting in Scotland: A Historical Bibliography* (2nd edition, 1976), *Accounting Thought and Education: Six English Pioneers* (1980), *Consolidation Accounting in Australia* (1983) and *Comparative International Accounting* (2nd edition, 1985); he is also the editor of *British Accountants: A Biographical Sourcebook* (1980) and *Bibliographies for Accounting Historians* (1980); co-editor of *Readings in the Concept and Measurement of Income* (2nd edition, 1986) and *The Evolution of Corporate Financial Reporting* (1979); and has published numerous articles in accounting and financial journals.

Since 1976 R. H. Parker has been Professor of Accountancy at the University of Exeter. He is joint editor of *Accounting and Business Research*, published by the Institute of Chartered Accountants in England and Wales. His main professional interests are in the international, comparative and historical aspects of accounting.

R. H. Parker

Understanding Company Financial Statements

Third Edition

Penguin Books

For Theresa and Michael

Acknowledgements

For 'The Hardship of Accounting' from *The Poetry of Robert Frost*, edited by Edward Connery Lathem: to the Estate of Robert Frost, Edward Connery Lathem and to Jonathan Cape Ltd. Copyright 1936 by Robert Frost. Copyright © 1964 by Lesley Frost Ballantine. Copyright © 1969 by Holt, Rinehart & Winston, Inc. Reprinted by permission of Holt, Rinehart & Winston, Inc.

PENGUIN BOOKS

Published by the Penguin Group
27 Wrights Lane, London w8 5TZ, England
Viking Penguin Inc., 40 West 23rd Street, New York, New York 10010, USA
Penguin Books Australia Ltd, Ringwood, Victoria, Australia
Penguin Books Canada Ltd, 2801 John Street, Markham, Ontario, Canada L3R 1B4
Penguin Books (NZ) Ltd, 182–190 Wairau Road, Auckland 10, New Zealand

Penguin Books Ltd, Registered Offices: Harmondsworth, Middlesex, England

First published 1972
Second edition 1982
Third edition 1988
10 9 8 7 6 5 4 3

Made and printed in Great Britain by
Richard Clay Ltd, Bungay, Suffolk
Filmset in Monophoto Sabon

Contents

Preface to the Third Edition

An eminent company lawyer has written of the published financial statements of companies that 'to the average investor or
creditor – "the man on the Clapham omnibus" – they are
cryptograms which he is incapable of solving'.* This small
book is an attempt to make the task easier. It is written for the
general reader and the first-year student, not for my fellow
accountants, and does not pretend to be more than an introduction to a difficult subject. No previous knowledge is assumed.
The emphasis is on analysis and interpretation rather than accounting techniques. Special attention has been paid to making
the language of accounting and finance intelligible to the layperson.

The first and second editions of this book were published in
1972 and 1982. The third retains the general approach of these
editions, but the pace of change has been so fast that much has
had to be rewritten.

I am greatly indebted to British Vita P L C for allowing me to
reprint its 1985 annual report and its 1986 interim report. I am
grateful to Mr R. H. Sellers and Mr S. McCann of British Vita,
to Mr R. S. O. Wallace and to others for valuable comments on
previous drafts of the manuscript, but any errors and mis-

* Gower, Cronin, Easson and Wedderburn, *Gower's Principles of Modern
Company Law* (Stevens, 4th edn, 1979), p. 507.

interpretations that may remain are, of course, my responsibility.

Over the years Mrs E. Ibbotson and Mrs H. Ireland have typed more versions of this book than either they or I care to remember. My thanks to them also.

1. Companies and Their Reports

In sooth a goodly company
REV. RICHARD HARRIS BARHAM, *The Jackdaw of Rheims*

Purpose and Design of the Book

The purpose of this book is to show the reader how to understand, analyse and interpret the reports sent by companies to their shareholders, and more especially the financial statements contained in them. In order to do this, we shall look in detail at the 1985 annual report of the British Vita group. We shall also refer occasionally to British Vita's 1984 and earlier reports and to the reports of other companies.

In this first chapter we survey in general terms the contents of a company annual report and look briefly at the nature and constitution of the limited liability company. Chapter 2 describes the various financial statements and introduces many important financial and accounting concepts. This is a vital chapter, providing the basis for the analysis which appears later in the book. Chapter 3 explains as briefly as possible the nature of company taxation and the function of the auditors. Chapter 4 deals with regulation, formats, accounting standards and inflation. Chapter 5 describes certain tools of analysis. Chapter 6 is concerned with profitability and return on investment, Chapter 7 with liquidity and cash flows, and Chapter 8 with sources of funds and capital structure. Chapter 9 summarizes the whole book.

Finance and accounting are specialist subjects. This does not mean that they need remain incomprehensible to the layperson.

It does mean, however, that technical terms cannot entirely be avoided. One would not, after all, learn to drive a car without learning words such as 'clutch' and 'accelerator'. In order to make the learning process as painless as possible, all technical terms are explained as they are introduced, and a glossary is provided for reference (Appendix B). It is hoped that some readers will want to know more about finance and accounting after reading this book. For such readers the references given in Chapter 9 should be useful.

Contents of a Company Annual Report

The 1985 annual report and accounts of British Vita PLC are reproduced as Appendix C by kind permission of the company. The original has a page size about twice that of the reproduction. The content of British Vita's report is typical of that of most listed companies. To get some idea of this content, it is worth leafing quickly through it.

What is the British Vita group and what do the member companies of it do? The group's own succinct description of itself is that the companies in the group are international leaders in foam, fibre, fabric and polymeric products. The principal activities listed in the directors' report [p. 8]* are

the manufacture of cellular foams, synthetic fibre fillings, specialized and coated fabrics, polymeric compounds and mouldings and a range of related consumer products. In addition, recent acquisitions have significantly extended the Group interests in licensing of advanced technical processes.

The section on Review of Operations [pp. 6–7] gives further details.

British Vita PLC of Middleton, near Manchester, is the parent company of the group. There are seven wholly owned subsidiaries operating in England, as well as fourteen European subsidiaries and three African subsidiaries [p. 26], in some of which there are minority shareholdings. The group also has numerous associated companies [p. 27].

* All references in square brackets are to pages in Appendix C.

Turning back to the beginning of the report, we find first of all the results for 1985 (with comparative figures for 1984) in the form of Financial Highlights, that is, in summarized form [p. 1]. Page 2 gives the names of the directors, the secretary, the auditors and the principal bankers. The company's official address ('registered office') is given, as is the name of its registrars (that is, the company appointed to handle transfers of the company's shares). Page 3 gives notice of the annual general meeting of the shareholders of the company. Every company must by law hold such a meeting once a year with an interval of not more than fifteen months between meetings.

The ordinary business of the meeting is very formal:

1   To receive and consider the accounts and reports of the directors and auditors for the year ended 31 December 1985.
2   To confirm the dividends paid and to declare a final dividend on the Ordinary shares [dividends are recommended by directors but approved and declared by the shareholders].
3   To re-elect a director.
4   To re-appoint auditors and authorize the directors to fix their remuneration.

There is also an item of special business.

The Chairman's Review appears on pages 4 and 5. Such a review, although not required by law, is published by almost all companies listed on the Stock Exchange. The content varies considerably. That of British Vita for 1985 looks both at the immediate past and at prospects for the future. Research has shown that this is one of the most widely read sections of an annual report, no doubt because it is presented in non-technical language and also, unlike most of the report, it deals with the future as well as the past.

The Directors' Report [pp. 8–9] is a statutory document whose contents are largely determined by law (there is a summary of the legal requirements in the Glossary). The main topics dealt with in British Vita's report are profit and dividends, principal activities, subsidiary companies, directors and other interests, share capital, fixed assets, close company provisions, personnel, donations and auditors.

Page 10 of the report gives a summary of financial information for the last five years. Page 11 contains the report of the auditors (see Chapter 3).

There now follows the most important and, for many, the most difficult section of the report: the financial statements. These consist of a consolidated profit and loss account, two balance sheets (one for the group and one for the parent company), a statement of group source and application of funds, a list of accounting policies (see Chapter 4) and ten pages of detailed notes. All of these will be looked at in detail later. For the moment it is enough to note that the consolidated profit and loss account shows the results of the operations of the British Vita *group of companies* for the year ended 31 December 1985; the group balance sheet shows the financial position of the *group* as at 31 December 1985; the parent balance sheet shows the financial position of the *parent company only* as at 31 December 1985; and the statement of source and application of funds shows the changes in the assets and liabilities of the *group* during the year ended 31 December 1985.

In previous annual reports, but not in 1985, British Vita has also published current cost information and a value added statement.

Users of Published Accounts

Although published financial statements are formally for share-holders only, they are also of great interest to other users. *The Corporate Report*, a discussion paper issued by the Accounting Standards Committee in 1975, classifies these other users as employees, loan creditors, analyst advisers, business contacts, the government and the public. It is British Vita's policy to make its annual report generally available and not to prepare statements specifically aimed at other users, especially as many of its employees are also shareholders. Many companies, however, prepare a special report for the employees (sometimes, but not always, distributed with the annual report). This report may emphasize the value added statement (see Chapters 2 and 6) rather than the profit and loss account.

Memorandum and Articles of Association

Every company must have both a memorandum of association and articles of association. The main contents of the memorandum are the name of the company, the situation of the registered office, a list of the objects for which the company has been formed, and a statement that the liability of the members is limited. The list of objects is important since a company cannot do anything which is beyond its powers (*ultra vires*). In practice the problem is avoided by listing every conceivable (and sometimes inconceivable) object that the company is ever likely to have.

The articles are the internal regulations of the company and usually deal with such matters as the rights of particular classes of shares, transfer of shares, powers and duties of directors, accounts, dividends, reserves and quorums for meetings of shareholders and directors. A model set of articles called Table A can be adopted in full or in a modified form.

Classification of Companies

In Britain the most important form of business organization is the limited liability company. The chief characteristics of such a company are a corporate personality distinct from that of its owners or shareholders; the limiting of the liability of the shareholders to the amount invested (which is not the case for a sole trader or partnership where personal assets are available to pay business debts); and, in principle at least, a perpetual life: companies are born but they do not have to die of old age.

It was not until 1844 that incorporation became possible other than by the slow and difficult process of a special Act of Parliament or a Royal Charter. It took another eleven years for incorporation by registration to be linked with limited liability by the Limited Liability Act 1855. The foundations of modern British company law (and also that of Australia, Canada, New Zealand, South Africa and many other Commonwealth or former Commonwealth countries) were laid in the Companies Act 1862. The law has been continually revised since. At the time of writing, most of the legislation in force is contained in the Companies Act 1985. The Commission of the European Communities has an active programme of company law harmonization which has increasingly affected British companies (see the section below on company law and the EEC).

At 31 March 1987 there were about 876,684 companies registered in Great Britain, of which 5,241, or 0·6 per cent, were 'public' companies and about 871,443 were 'private' companies. In 1986–7, 115,674 new companies were registered with a nominal capital of £5,458 million.*

To explain the differences between public and private companies it is necessary to look at the ways in which companies can be classified. Since 1981 a public company has been one whose memorandum of association states that it is such, whose name ends with the words 'public limited company' or 'plc' (or, optionally, 'ccc' for companies registered in Wales) and which has a minimum authorized and allotted share capital, one quarter at least of which has been paid up. The minimum amount is set at present at £50,000. Any company which is not a public company is a private company. A private company is not permitted to issue shares or debentures to the public.

A public company does not *have* to make a public issue of shares or debentures; it simply has the right to do so. Thus only about 2,100 public companies are listed (quoted) on a stock exchange and the division between private and public companies is not the same as that between companies with listed shares and those with unlisted shares. It is a necessary but not a sufficient condition for listing that the company be a public company. British Vita PLC is both a public and a listed company.

The Companies Act 1985 also divides companies into large, medium and small, using as criteria balance sheet total, turnover and the average number of employees. Small and medium companies are exempted from filing certain data with the Registrar of Companies. The exemptions do not apply to financial statements sent to shareholders.

All companies must have at least two shareholders; there is no maximum limit. At 31 March 1987, for example, British

* Department of Trade and Industry, *Companies in 1986–7* (HMSO, 1987).

	1963 %	1969 %	1975 %	1981 %
Persons	54·0	47·4	37·5	28·2
Charities	2·1	2·1	2·3	2·2
Banks	1·3	1·7	0·7	0·3
Insurance companies	10·0	12·2	15·9	20·5
Pension funds	6·4	9·0	16·8	26·7
Unit trusts	1·3	2·9	4·1	3·6
Investment trusts and other financial companies	11·3	10·1	10·5	6·8
Industrial and commercial companies	5·1	5·4	3·0	5·1
Public sector	1·5	2·6	3·6	3·0
Overseas sector	7·0	6·6	5·6	3·6
	100·0	100·0	100·0	100·0

Source: *The Stock Exchange Survey of Share Ownership*, Table 2.1b.

Telecom had 1,417,905 ordinary shareholders.* Not all share-holders are persons. Given above are estimates of percentages of market value of shareholdings by sector of *beneficial* holder. Since shares can be held by a nominee, the beneficial holder is not necessarily the same as the registered holder of a share.

The features to note are the steady fall in the percentage of shares held by persons and the steady rise in the holding of financial companies and institutions (pension funds, insurance companies, investment trusts, unit trusts and banks).

Some companies voluntarily disclose shareholder statistics. These may sometimes be difficult to interpret because of the existence of nominee shareholdings. At 31 December 1986, for example, BICC plc had 209 million ordinary shares and 35,815 ordinary shareholders (that is, the *average* holding was about 5,850 shares). The average institutional shareholding, however, was about 28,080 shares while the average individual holding was about 1,030 shares. Only 17·8 per cent of the shareholders

* The distinction between shareholders and stockholders, and between shares and stock, is not of practical importance. The terms are increasingly used interchangeably.

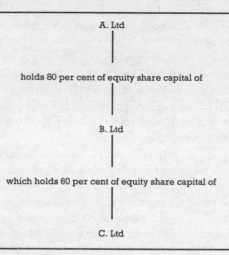

A. Ltd

holds 80 per cent of equity share capital of

B. Ltd

which holds 60 per cent of equity share capital of

C. Ltd

were institutions (banks, unit trusts, nominee companies, pension funds and investment trusts), but they held 85.4 per cent of the shares. Shareholdings of 5 per cent or over must be reported to a company by law. British Vita reports [p. 9] that apart from certain directors only the Legal and General Assurance Society held more than 5 per cent of its issued share capital as at 25 February 1986.

Companies can take the power, and nearly always do so, to hold shares in other companies. A 'holding company' and a 'subsidiary company' exist where *either* the former is a shareholder of the latter *and* controls the composition of the latter's board of directors; *or* the former holds more than half in nominal value of the latter's equity share capital. An 'associated company' is one in which 50 per cent or less of the shares are held and over which a significant influence is exercised. It is possible for a subsidiary itself to have subsidiaries. These are the sub-subsidiaries of the first holding company. In the example above, A. Ltd is a holding company, B. Ltd a subsidiary, and C. Ltd a sub-subsidiary.

Note that A. Ltd's interest in C. Ltd is only 48 per cent, i.e., 80 per cent of 60 per cent.

Some holding companies exist purely to hold shares in operating subsidiaries. Others, like British Vita PLC, are operating companies as well

The holding–subsidiary relationship is very common and practically all the annual reports which the reader is likely to be interested in will be those of *groups* of companies. It is possible for subsidiaries to hold shares in each other, but the Companies Act makes it illegal, with minor exceptions, for a subsidiary to hold shares in its holding company.

The annual reports with which we shall be concerned, then, will be those of groups or sub-groups of companies. The holding company will usually be a public one. Other members of the group will be British public or private companies or companies incorporated overseas.* All those concerned will have share capital. It is worth noting in passing that not all companies do have share capital. Some are 'limited by guarantee' (that is, the members have undertaken to contribute a fixed amount to the assets of the company in the event of its being wound up). The London School of Economics and Political Science is an example. Some companies are even unlimited; since these have the privilege of not publishing their accounts, they are not relevant to this book. They are used by professionals who desire corporate form but are not permitted to limit their liability, or by those who value the privilege of non-publication more than the limitation of liability (for example, the C & A department store). They have become more important since the Companies Act 1967 abolished 'exempt private companies' (essentially family companies exempt from publishing their accounts).

Company Law and the EEC

The EEC's active programme of company law harmonization means that British company law will be further amended in the

---

* The American equivalent of plc and Ltd is Inc. (i.e., incorporated). The nearest French, German and Dutch equivalents to a British public company are a *société anonyme* (SA), an *Aktiengesellschaft* (AG) and a *Naamloze Venootschap* (NV); to our private companies, *société à responsabilité limitée* (SARL), *Gesellschaft mit beschränkter Haftung* (GmbH) and *Besloten Venootschap* (BV).

near future. The Council of Ministers of the EEC has adopted a series of company law 'directives' which each member state has to incorporate into its own legislation. The most important so far as company financial reporting is concerned are the fourth and the seventh. The former introduced into Britain standardized formats for financial statements (see Chapter 2) and a three tier classification into large, medium and small companies. The latter deals with consolidated financial statements and has not yet been implemented in the UK.

Interim Reports

Twelve months is a long time to wait for information about the details of the financial progress of a company. It has therefore become increasingly common for major companies to issue unaudited interim reports at half-yearly and sometimes quarterly intervals. Listed companies are required by the Stock Exchange to circularize a half-yearly interim report to shareholders not later than six months from the date of the notice calling an annual general meeting. Companies with exceptionally large numbers of shareholders are allowed to insert such interim reports instead in two leading London newspapers (for example, the *Financial Times* and *The Times*), or in one such newspaper and one provincial newspaper.

British Vita's interim report for the six months ended 30 June 1986 is reproduced in Appendix D. It comprises a chairman's statement, a group profit and loss account with comparative figures, and details of earnings and dividends per share. It also carries details of a proposed increase in authorized share capital and a capitalization issue (see Chapter 8).

Annual Financial Statements

It is, however, with the annual financial statements that this book is mainly concerned. Now that we have sufficient background information, we can look at them in more detail.

2. The Financial Statements

The statements was interesting but tough
MARK TWAIN, *The Adventures of Huckleberry Finn*, Ch. 17

Assets, Liabilities and Shareholders' Funds

At the core of any company's annual report are the financial statements. Those for the British Vita group for the year ended 31 December 1985 are reproduced as Appendix C. We shall start by discussing the 1985 group balance sheet (the column of figures furthest to the left on page 13 of the appendix). This is a statement of the financial position of British Vita and its subsidiaries at 31 December 1985 as if they were one company.

Traditionally, British companies have had the right to present a balance sheet in any way they please, so long as certain items are disclosed either on the face of the balance sheet or in the notes. As a result of the EEC's fourth directive on company accounts, balance sheets are now more standardized in form (see Chapter 4). All company balance sheets, however, are built up from three main categories, namely, assets, liabilities and shareholders' funds. The relationship between these three items can be looked at either from the point of view of shareholders (a 'proprietary' approach) or from the point of view of the company as a whole (an 'entity' approach). Two forms of the fundamental balance sheet identity can thus be derived:

Proprietary: assets − liabilities = shareholders' funds
Entity: assets = shareholders' funds + liabilities

In less technical language, all that is being said is that, firstly, what a company owns *less* what a company owes is equal to the value of the shareholders' funds invested in it and that, secondly, what a company owns is financed partly by the owners (the shareholders) and partly by outsiders (the liabilities). Either way, a balance sheet must, by definition, balance. The useful accounting technique known as double entry ('debits' and 'credits') is based on these same identities (see Appendix A).

As we shall see in the next few sections, the three categories can each be subdivided: e.g., shareholders' funds into share capital and reserves; assets into fixed assets and current assets; and liabilities into current liabilities (i.e., creditors falling due within one year), creditors falling due after more than one year, and provisions for liabilities and charges.

British Vita has adopted an entity approach and presents its consolidated balance sheet in the following form [p. 13]:

	£000
Fixed assets	53,423
Current assets	74,801
Creditors: amounts falling due within one year	(64,854)
Net current assets	9,947
Total assets less current liabilities	63,370
Creditors: amounts falling due after more than one year	15,256
Provisions for liabilities and charges	1,477
Minority interests	566
Capital and reserves	46,071
Capital employed	63,370

The total assets less current liabilities (or, more briefly, net assets) are shown to be financed by the parent company shareholders (the capital and reserves item), by various borrowings and, to a very small extent, by the minority shareholders in the subsidiary companies.

The second important financial statement is the consolidated profit and loss account [p. 12]. It will be noted that while a balance sheet is for a particular moment, a profit and loss account (the American phrase is income statement) is for a period, in this case for the year ended 31 December 1985. It shows, from the point of view of the shareholders, the results of the year's activities. The British Vita group made sales (turnover) in 1985 of approximately £186·1 million. The operating profit was £11,790,000; after addition of the share of profit of associated companies and deduction of interest this figure rose to £12,231,000 (profit on ordinary activities before taxation). This was reduced by taxation to £7,156,000 (profit on ordinary activities after taxation). After allowing for minority interests and extraordinary items the profit for the year available for the shareholders came to £3,717,000. Out of this amount dividends have been or will be paid to the shareholders amounting altogether to £2,116,000. This leaves £1,601,000 to be retained (ploughed back).

The group profit and loss account is drawn up from the point of view of the shareholders. A rather different view of the same figures can be gained by preparing a statement of value added. Unlike the profit and loss account, this statement is not required by law. The philosophy behind it is that the group by its activities creates new wealth ('adds value') which is then shared out among the employees, the providers of capital and the government, with a balance being retained to provide for the maintenance and expansion of assets.

Although British Vita, like many other companies, no longer publishes a statement of value added, it is possible to derive one so long as wages and salaries are disclosed. The necessary calculations are shown in Chapter 6. The statement given there demonstrates that gross value added was applied in 1985 as follows (p. 14).

It is worth looking more closely at the link between the profit and loss account and the balance sheet. How can a company grow – that is, how can it increase its assets? Look again at the identity

---

assets = liabilities + shareholders' funds.

It is clear that the only ways to increase the assets are to increase

	%
Employees	72
Providers of capital:	
interest	4
dividends to British Vita shareholders	4
minority shareholders	0
Governments (as taxation)	8
Retentions for replacement and expansion:	
depreciation	9
retained profit	3
	100

the liabilities (to borrow) or to increase the shareholders' funds. How can a company increase the latter? There are two possibilities: it can issue more shares or it can plough back profits (assuming, of course, it is making some). Ploughing back profits is the simplest but not necessarily the cheapest source of long-term finance for a company. Also, the more a company ploughs back the less, in the short run at least, there will be available for paying dividends.

The sources and uses of funds of a company for a period are shown in a statement of source and application of funds (sometimes known more briefly as a funds statement). In 1985 the British Vita group [p. 14] generated funds of £12,768,000 from operations and funds from other sources (notably loans) of £6,687,000. These were used, *inter alia*, to purchase tangible fixed assets (£9,568,000), repay creditors (£6,566,000), acquire subsidiaries (£5,786,000), pay taxation (£3,193,000) and pay dividends (£1,962,000).

By using simple algebra it is possible to show quite clearly the links between the balance sheet, the profit and loss account and the funds statement. The following symbols will be used:

a = assets	r = revenue (e.g., sales, fees)
l = liabilities	e = expenses other than taxation
c = shareholders' funds	t = taxation
s = share capital	d = dividends
p = retained or ploughed back profits (reserves)	Δ = net increase in

The identity for any balance sheet will then be

$$a = l + c$$

which can be expanded to

$$a = l + s + p \tag{i}$$

The statement of source and application of funds shows the net increase in each item and can therefore be written as

$$\Delta a = \Delta l + \Delta s + \Delta p \tag{ii}$$

The profit and loss account is merely an expansion of the last item on the right-hand side (Δp, or net increase in retained profits). The equation is

$$p = r - e - t - d \tag{iii}$$

Equation (ii) can therefore be expanded to read

$$a = l + s + r - e - t - d \tag{iv}$$

For those who dislike algebra these four equations and their relationships are shown in the diagrams on page 16. It should be noted that the relative proportions of liabilities and shareholders' funds have changed, although, of course, the sum of the two categories must by definition be equal to the assets.

Current Assets, Current Liabilities and Working Capital

Current assets are those assets which either are in the form of cash or can reasonably be expected to be turned into cash within one year from the date of the balance sheet. The British Vita group at 31 December 1985 had current assets valued at £74,801,000, comprising stocks ('inventories' in US terminology) of £22,241,000, debtors ('accounts receivable') of £46,716,000 and cash at bank and in hand of £5,844,000. The figure for

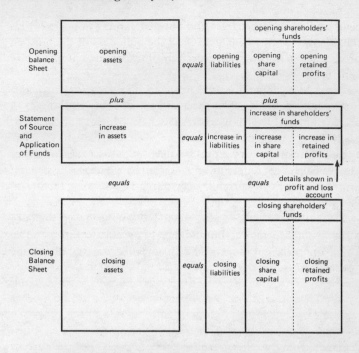

stocks may vary according to the rules of valuation adopted. British Vita's policy is set out as follows [p. 15]:

Stocks are valued at the lower of first-in, first-out cost and net realizable value; cost includes appropriate production overhead expenses.

The use of the lower of cost or net realizable value (that is, expected selling price net of selling expenses) is standard practice in Britain. The phrase first-in, first-out (FIFO) refers to the assumption that the stocks acquired first have been sold or used up first. An alternative assumption, last-in, first-out (LIFO), is popular in the USA but rare in Britain. The cost of finished goods includes not only raw materials and direct labour but also production overheads (but not administrative or selling overheads). In note 14 [p. 22], the group's stocks are analysed into raw materials and consumable stores on the one hand (64 per cent) and work in progress and finished goods (36 per cent) on the other. These percentages reflect the bulkiness of the finished products, stocks of which, especially of the parent company, are kept at a minimum.

The debtors figure is usually net of an allowance (or provision) for doubtful debts. Cash at bank and in hand may be thought to present no problem, but where it is held overseas and cannot easily be remitted its value may be doubted. British Vita has excluded from its 1985 group balance sheet the cash and other assets held by its Zambian subsidiary [pp. 16, 22]. The general problem of foreign currency accounting is discussed further in Chapter 4.

Current liabilities are also described in the group balance sheet as creditors: amounts falling due within one year. The group's current liabilities of £64,854,000 at 31 December 1985 are analysed in note 17 [p. 22]. The most important are trade creditors (i.e., amounts owing to suppliers) of £35,857,000, bank overdrafts of £10,001,000, corporation tax of £2,857,000, other taxes and social security costs of £4,073,000 and the proposed dividend of £1,118,000. The total of current liabilities when deducted from the current assets of £74,801,000 gives net current assets of £9,947,000. Net current assets are also referred to as net working capital, or (more usually) just working capital. The relationship between current assets and current liabilities is very important and is discussed in detail in Chapter 7 on liquidity.

Fixed Assets

Fixed assets comprise those assets which are intended for use on a continuing basis for the purpose of the company's activities. Stocks, for example, are not regarded as fixed assets since they are acquired either for immediate resale (for example, cigarettes, as sold by a tobacconist) or as raw materials for use in manufacturing operations, or are the finished or partly finished ('work in progress') results of such operations. It will be seen from the group balance sheet and notes 12 and 13 [pp. 20–21] that the net book values of the fixed assets of the British Vita group at 31 December 1985 were as follows:

	£000	
Tangible fixed assets:		
land	4,395	
buildings	16,645	
plant & vehicles	19,994	
		41,034
Investments in:		
subsidiary companies	649	
listed associated companies	5,841	
unlisted associated companies	5,899	
		12,389
Total		53,423

Tangible Fixed Assets

British Vita's fixed assets are of two kinds: tangible fixed assets and investments. Note 12 [p. 20] reveals that some fixed assets are shown at cost and some at a valuation made in 1984. 'Cost' in accounting has usually meant the historical cost of acquisition or manufacture (if the asset was made by the company for its own use). Historical cost has been favoured by accountants because it is thought to be objective and verifiable by an independent third party such as an auditor. It can, however, get seriously out of line with current market values, especially in times of inflation. British Vita discloses that, had their land and buildings not been revalued, they would have been stated in the group balance sheet at a net book value of £16,970,000 instead of £24,715,000.

It should be noted that it is intention that determines whether an asset is fixed or not. Plant and vehicles, for example, would be the *current* assets of a company whose business it was to manufacture them for sale.

In accordance with the Companies Act, British Vita provides a breakdown of its land and buildings into freehold, long leasehold and short leasehold.

Depreciation

The concept of depreciation means different things to different people, but in an accounting context it normally means spreading the net cost (sometimes after adjustment or revaluation) of a fixed asset over its estimated useful economic life. British Vita explains its policy as follows [p. 15]:

> Depreciation of tangible fixed assets is provided at rates estimated to write off the cost or valuation of assets over their useful lives, the principal rates of annual straight line depreciation being:
> (a) Freehold buildings $2\frac{1}{2}$%.
> (b) Leasehold land and buildings $2\frac{1}{2}$% or over the period of the lease if less than forty years.
> (c) Plant between 10% and $33\frac{1}{3}$%.
> (d) Vehicles between 16% and 25%.

British Vita thus uses the straight line method of depreciation. Under this method the cost less estimated scrap value of a fixed asset is divided by the number of years of its estimated useful life. If, for example, a machine costs £1,200 and is expected to have a scrap value of £130 at the end of an estimated useful life of ten years, the annual depreciation using this method will be £1,070 ÷ 10 = £107.

Less popular but still quite common in Britain is the reducing balance method of depreciation. As the name implies, the amount of depreciation charged each year under this method decreases over the life of the asset. If, for example, a rate of 20 per cent were chosen for the asset which costs £1,200, the annual depreciation charges would be calculated as shown on p. 20.

The machine has been written down to its approximate scrap value. The correct percentage can be found by trial and error or by use of the formula

$$1 - \sqrt[n]{\frac{s}{c}}$$

where n is the number of years, s the estimated scrap value and c the cost. In this case

		£
Cost		1,200
Year 1	Depreciation 20% of £1,200	240
		960
Year 2	Depreciation 20% of £960	192
		768
Year 3	Depreciation 20% of £768	154
		614
Year 4	Depreciation 20% of £614	123
		491
Year 5	Depreciation 20% of £491	98
		393
Year 6	Depreciation 20% of £393	79
		314
Year 7	Depreciation 20% of £314	63
		251
Year 8	Depreciation 20% of £251	50
		201
Year 9	Depreciation 20% of £201	40
		161
Year 10	Depreciation 20% of £161	32
		£129

$$1 - \sqrt[10]{\frac{130}{1200}} = 0{\cdot}2$$

The charging of depreciation simultaneously reduces the recorded amount of the fixed asset and reduces net profit.

For the year ended 31 December 1985 the group charged against profits £4,850,000 of depreciation. The amounts given for the fixed assets in the group balance sheet are net of all accumulated depreciation, not only that of the current year but of all previous years since the purchase of the assets concerned.

Fixed Asset Investments

British Vita has a substantial investment in associated companies. Associated companies are usually also related companies as defined in the Companies Act 1985 [p. 15]. The shares of these are valued at cost less amounts written off in the company's own books, but this is increased in the group balance sheet to include a proportionate share of their reserves (retained profits) since acquisition. This accounting treatment, which differs from that used for a subsidiary, is known as the 'equity method'.

Like associated companies, the shares of subsidiaries in a parent company balance sheet are valued at cost less amounts written off. The shares of most subsidiaries, however, are eliminated from group balance sheets and replaced by their underlying assets and liabilities. Subsidiaries may be excluded from consolidation for a number of reasons, including difficulties in remitting profits to the holding company. When so excluded, their shares are valued at cost less amounts written off [p. 16].

Intangible Fixed Assets

A third category of fixed asset, which is not represented in British Vita's balance sheet, is the intangible fixed asset. This category includes not only such 'identifiable' intangibles as patents, trade marks and copyrights (see Glossary), but also goodwill.

A company is not just a collection of tangible assets. It is, or should be, a going concern whose total value, by reason of its proven ability to earn profits, is greater than the sum of its parts. It is the difference between the total value and the sum of the parts which constitutes goodwill. It should not be regarded as in any way a fictitious asset: to be valuable, an asset does not have to be tangible. Goodwill is, however, very difficult to value objectively and it is for this reason that it does not appear in a balance sheet unless it has been purchased, and even then it is written off either immediately or quite quickly. This explains why British Vita's group balance sheet does not include any goodwill derived from the balance sheets of the individual companies in the group. In some group balance sheets, however, an item appears entitled 'goodwill arising on consolidation' or 'goodwill on acquisition'. This represents the excess of the cost of shares in subsidiary companies over the book value of their net tangible assets at the date of acquisition, i.e., the parent company was willing to pay more to purchase a company than the sum of its tangible fixed and net current assets. British Vita writes off goodwill on acquisition to distributable reserves [p. 15, para. 2].

Loan Capital

The item 'Creditors: amounts falling due after more than one year' in British Vita's group balance sheet represents the extent to which the group, not wishing to obtain further long-term funds from its shareholders, has borrowed from outsiders, both in the UK and overseas. Details are given in notes 17 and 18 [pp. 22–3]. The major part consists of loans both long-term (not wholly repayable within five years) and medium-term (repayable within five years). The proportion of the loans payable within one year is included under the heading 'Creditors: amounts falling due within one year'.

The loans are shown under various names: debenture stock, bank loan and loan notes. The word 'debenture' simply refers to a document evidencing a long-term borrowing or loan. Debentures are usually, but not necessarily, secured on the assets of the company, in which case they may be known as mortgage debentures. If a company fails in its obligation to pay interest or repay the loan, certain property of the company can be sold in order to provide the necessary funds. The phrase 'unsecured debenture' is unusual, 'unsecured loan' being preferred in practice. 'Debenture stock' means that instead of issuing individual debentures the company has created one loan fund to be divided among a class of lenders, each of whom will receive a debenture stock certificate. Companies may, and often do, make more than one issue of debentures, the terms of issue and, in particular, the rate of interest varying according to the financial circumstances of the time. Such issues may be made at par (that is, at face value), at a discount (less than face value) or at a premium (more than face value). Issue at a discount increases the effective interest rate payable; issue at a premium (rare) reduces it. Issues are often made at a discount in order to keep the interest rate on the par value (known as the coupon rate) a reasonably round figure, while allowing the effective rate to be adjusted more finely.

Debentures and loans may be secured by a fixed charge on a particular asset or by a floating charge on all the assets or particular classes of assets. A floating charge, unlike a fixed charge, allows a company to dispose of the assets charged in the usual course of business without obtaining special permission from the lender. Stock-in-trade is a particularly suitable asset to be charged in this manner. If assets are, or may be, used as security for more than one loan, it is necessary to state the order of priority of the lenders (for example, debenture stock may be stated to be secured by a *first* floating charge).

Some debentures are irredeemable – that is, they will never have to be repaid (unless the company is wound up) – but most are redeemable. It is common not only to specify the latest date, but also to give the company the power to redeem earlier if it so wishes. This is especially useful if debentures are issued in times of high interest rates and if there is an expectation of lower rates later.

How much loan capital to issue, and when and in what form to issue it, are vital matters to any company. We shall look at these problems in Chapter 8.

Provisions for Liabilities and Charges

Provisions for liabilities and charges are defined as amounts retained as reasonably necessary for the purpose of providing for any liability or loss which is either likely to be incurred, or certain to be incurred, but uncertain as to amount or as to the date on which it will arise. The two most important provisions of this kind are for deferred taxation and for pensions. Deferred taxation is discussed in Chapter 3.

Share Capital and Reserves

The shareholders' funds section of the group balance sheet is sub-divided into share capital and reserves. Further details are given in notes 20, 21, 22, 23 and 24 [pp. 24–5].

Shareholders differ from debenture-holders in that they are members (owners) of the company, not lenders, in that they receive dividends (a share of the profits), not interest, and in that, except in special circumstances, the cost of their shares will not be repaid to them by their company. Listed shares can of course be sold on a stock exchange, but both the redemption of shares and the buying back of a company of its own shares, although possible subject to certain restrictions, are relatively uncommon in the UK.

There are two main types of shares: ordinary and preference. The difference between an ordinary shareholder and a preference shareholder is very important. The latter is usually entitled only to a dividend at a fixed rate (4·2 per cent in the case of British Vita), but has priority of repayment in the event of the company being wound up. This is not always so, however, and the exact rights must always be looked up in the company's articles of association. Preference shares may be cumulative or non-cumulative. British Vita's are cumulative, which means that if the company misses a dividend payment it carries it forward to the next year. Any arrears of preference dividends must be shown in a note to the balance sheet. Non-cumulative preference dividends, on the other hand, do not have to be carried forward.

The ordinary shareholder is not entitled to a fixed dividend, the size varying according to the profits made by the company. It can be seen from the Directors' Report [p. 8] that an interim ordinary dividend of 3·3p per share was paid during 1985 and that a final ordinary dividend of 3·7p is proposed. The total ordinary dividend is thus 7·0p. The par or face value of the ordinary shares is 25p each [p. 24, note 20], and the total dividend could be described as a dividend of 28 per cent on the par value.

More important to an investor is the relationship between the dividend and the current *market* price of the share. This is known as the dividend yield and is discussed in Chapter 8 in the context of earnings yields and price-earnings ratios. For the moment, it should be noted that every share must have a par value* but that this is not necessarily the same as the issue price of the shares or their market price. Shares can be issued at more than their par value: this gives rise to a *share premium*. The British Vita group has a share premium of £4,607,000 [p. 21, note 21]. A share premium cannot be distributed, but it can be used to make a bonus or capitalization issue (see p. 96). Once a share has been issued, its market price fluctuates from day to day in accordance with supply and demand. If the shares can be bought and sold on a stock exchange, then the current market price can easily be obtained from the financial pages of a newspaper or from the *Stock Exchange Daily Official List*. The most complete newspaper list is given in the *Financial Times*. The information given in that paper's daily share information service is further discussed in Chapter 8.

A company does not have to issue all its shares at once, nor does it have to request full payment on the shares immediately. British Vita has authority to issue (that is, it has authorized capital of) 38,000,000 ordinary shares of 25p each, and 60,000 4·2 per cent cumulative preference shares of £1 each [p. 24, note 20]. As at 31 December 1985 it had issued 30,200,302 ordinary shares (par value £7,550,075) and 57,000 preference shares (par value £57,000). All the shares are described as being fully paid; that is, the company does not have the right to call up any further amounts from the shareholders. They could have been partly paid. For example, a 25p share could be payable 5p on application for the shares, a further 5p on allotment when the directors decide to whom the shares are going to be issued (or 'allotted'), and the remaining 15p in calls. Thus, in summary, one can distinguish authorized, issued, called-up and paid-up share capital.

In 1985 British Vita increased its issued share capital by allotting 72,275 ordinary shares, fully paid, under employee share schemes. It did not increase its authorized share capital.

Details of the group's reserves are given in notes 21, 22, 23 and 24 [pp. 24–5]. The Companies Act distinguishes between 'distributable' and 'undistributable' reserves. The former comprises realized profits less realized losses. British Vita's profit

* No-par-value shares are common in North America but illegal in the UK.

and loss account balance of £23,128,000 comes into this category. Its share premium account, revaluation reserve (created as a result of the revaluation of fixed assets on the other side of the balance sheet) and other reserves, totalling altogether £15,336,000, are regarded by the company as undistributable.

It is very important not to confuse reserves with cash. To say that a company has large reserves is not the same thing as saying that it has plenty of cash. If a company has reserves it must have net assets of equal amount, but these assets may be of any kind (e.g., machinery, stock-in-trade). Thus it is perfectly possible (and often sensible) for a company to have both large reserves and a large bank overdraft.

Consolidated Profit and Loss Account

British Vita's consolidated profit and loss account is given on page 12 of its annual report. It follows the most popular of the four formats permitted by the Companies Act (see Chapter 4) and summarizes the year's operations from the point of view of the shareholders. As already noted, a statement of value added (see Chapter 6) shows these operations from a wider viewpoint.

The first item in the profit and loss account is turnover (£186,108,000). This represents the net amounts invoiced to external customers but excludes value added taxes and sales taxes and the sales of the associated companies [p. 15]. Turnover within the group is not included, since to do so would merely inflate both sales and purchases. Note 3 [p. 17] analyses turnover by major business groupings and by geographical market. The figures show substantial increases in sales to continental Europe.

Cost of sales (£144,144,000) – that is, the cost of the goods sold during 1985 whether or not manufactured in 1985 – is deducted from turnover to give the gross profit (£41,964,000). From this are further deducted distribution costs (£10,434,000) and administrative expenses (£19,740,000) to give an operating profit of £11,790,000. Some of the more important constituents of cost of sales, distribution costs and administrative expenses are disclosed in notes 4 [p. 17] and 11 [p. 19]. From these we can discover total employment costs (£40,131,000), broken down into wages and salaries, social security costs and other pension costs, depreciation (£4,850,000) and the cost of leasing of plant and vehicles (£719,000). Vehicles and plant may be leased instead of owned (see Chapter 8). Either way, the group has the use of them – hence the law also requires disclosure of leasing charges. Details are also given of the directors' emoluments and the auditors' remuneration (see Chapter 3).

The next item is the group share of profits of associated companies. The accounting treatment of associated companies differs, as we have seen, from that of subsidiaries. Like the latter, the appropriate share of profit or loss before tax is brought into the group results and not just dividends received; but, unlike the latter, it is brought in as one figure, not split into its component parts. British Vita discloses in note 5 [p. 17] both its share of the profits of its associated companies (£1,655,000) and dividends receivable from them (£631,000). In the balance sheet, it will be remembered, the underlying assets and liabilities of an associated company are *not* brought in, but instead the cost of the original investment is augmented by a share of the associated company's retained profits since acquisition.

The next item is interest (net) of £2,143,000, further details of which are given, in accordance with the Companies Act, in note 6 [p. 17].

It is now possible to calculate profit on ordinary activities before taxation (£12,231,000). Taxation (see Chapter 3) amounts to £5,075,000, so profit on ordinary activities after taxation is £7,156,000.

The profit after tax is not the same as the profit for the year attributable to shareholders. Two more items need to be deducted. These are the share of the profit after tax which is attributable to the minority shareholders in the subsidiary companies in the group (£70,000 in 1985) and the 'extraordinary' items (£3,369,000 in 1985). Standard accounting practice distinguishes between extraordinary items, exceptional items and prior year adjustments. *Extraordinary items* are those which derive from events or transactions outside the ordinary activities of a business and which are both material and expected not to recur frequently or regularly. *Exceptional items* derive from the ordinary activities of the business. *Prior year adjustments* are material adjustments applicable to prior years arising from changes in accounting policies or from the correction of fundamental errors. Extraordinary items can be profits or losses and are shown net of tax. British Vita's in 1985 comprised closure and restructuring costs, the loss on realization of assets blocked in Zambia, and the profit on disposal of associated companies.

We have at last reached the profit for the year attributable to shareholders. This amounted to £3,717,000 in 1985. The remainder of the profit and loss account is concerned with the distribution or retention of this sum: £2,116,000 has been or will be distributed; £1,601,000 is to be retained. Details of dividends are given in note 9 [p. 19]. An interim dividend of £996,000 has already been distributed to the ordinary shareholders. A final dividend of £1,118,000 is proposed. The preference shareholders receive £2,000.

The profits retained are spread around the group: £376,000 in the books of the holding company, £201,000 in the books of the subsidiaries and £1,024,000 in the books of the associated companies (over whose dividend payment policies British Vita has significant influence but not control).

At the foot of the group profit and loss account a note is given of the earnings per ordinary share. Earnings per share (EPS) is based on earnings per *ordinary* share and *before* extraordinary items. The relevant figure for earnings was thus £7,084,000 in 1985. EPS is not of interest to preference shareholders since their dividend is fixed irrespective of the level of earnings. The inclusion of extraordinary items would distort year-to-year comparisons.

As at 31 December 1985 there were 30,200,302 shares [p. 24]. The EPS calculation is, however, based on the weighted average of ordinary shares in issue during the year, namely, 30,138,283 shares [note 10, p. 19]. The calculation of EPS is thus:

$$\text{EPS} = \frac{7,084,000 \times 100}{30,138,283}\,\text{p} = 23.5\text{p}$$

The concept of earnings per share is discussed further in Chapter 8.

Profit earned needs to be related to investment made and compared, if possible, with the performance of similar companies. Profitability and return on investment form the main subjects of Chapter 6.

Statement of Source and Application of Funds (Funds Statement)

It will be remembered that a funds statement shows *changes* during the year in assets, liabilities, share capital and retained profits, and that the last item is made up of revenues less expenses (including depreciation), less tax and less dividends. British Vita group's statement of Source and Application of Funds for the year ended 31 December 1985 is given on page 14 of Appendix C.

In summary terms the sources and application of funds (arranged in order of importance) were as follows:

	£000	%
Sources		
Total funds generated from operations (mainly composed of profit before tax after adding back depreciation)	12,768	66
Increase in loans	5,361	27
Sale of tangible fixed assets	534	3
Issue of ordinary share capital	86	0
Other sources	706	4
	19,455	100
Uses (Applications)		
Purchase of tangible fixed assets	9,568	49
Acquisition of subsidiaries	5,786	30
Tax paid	3,193	17
Dividends paid	1,962	10
Other uses	819	4
Working capital movement excluding cash (i.e., stock + debtors − creditors)	(8,120)	(42)
	13,208	68
Increase in net cash balances	6,247	32
	19,455	100

By far the most important source of funds for the British Vita group in 1985 was that generated from its own operations (66 per cent). Less important were an increase in loans (27 per cent), the sale of tangible fixed assets (3 per cent) and the issue of ordinary share capital (less than 1 per cent). The increase in ordinary share capital was a result of the share option scheme and not really an attempt to raise funds for expansion.

The most important uses of funds were the purchase of tangible fixed assets (49 per cent), the acquisition of subsidiaries (30 per cent), tax (17 per cent) and dividends (10 per cent). The assets and liabilities acquired on the acquisition of subsidiaries are given in a note to the funds statement. The tax and dividend figures are not the same as those in the group profit and loss account, but represent tax *paid* and dividends *paid*. The latter figure (£1,962,000) is easily checked. It is equal to the proposed ordinary dividends of 1984 (£964,000) plus 1985's interim ordinary dividend of £996,000 and preference dividend of £2,000.

Depreciation as a 'Source' of Funds

Depreciation is sometimes described as a 'source' of funds. It will be noted that the British Vita group has been careful not to do this. The depreciation for the year of £4,850,000 is shown in the statement of source and application of funds as the largest of several 'items not involving the movement of funds'.

Depreciation is in fact neither a source nor an application (use) of funds. The use of funds obviously took place when the fixed asset was originally bought. It would be double counting to regard each year's depreciation as a further use, and the relevant profit figure in the statement of source and application of funds is therefore *profit before charging depreciation* (but after charging wages, etc.). But the same arithmetical result can be reached by adding back depreciation to profit *after* charging depreciation. This is quite commonly done, but it should not mislead us into thinking that funds can be obtained merely by increasing the depreciation charge in the books.* If, for example, British Vita group's depreciation had

* The change in the depreciation charge would not affect the tax payable (see Chapter 3).

been £4,950,000 instead of £4,850,000, then its profit before taxation would have been £12,131,000 instead of £12,231,000 and its total sources of funds would have remained unchanged.

Cash Flow

Cash flow is a term popular with financial analysts rather than accountants. It is often used rather imprecisely, but is usually defined as net profit plus depreciation and other items not involving the movement of funds. A more accurate name for cash flow in this sense is 'total funds generated from operations'. A study of British Vita's source and application of funds statement should make it clear why this figure is different from the change in net cash balances.

Events after the Balance Sheet Date

Important events may sometimes take place between the date of the balance sheet (e.g., 31 December 1985) and the date on which the balance sheet is approved by the board of directors for publication (e.g., 7 March 1986). An event which does not provide additional evidence of conditions existing at the balance sheet date (e.g., the acquisition of a new subsidiary) is known as a 'non-adjusting event'. An example of an 'adjusting event', one which would require the financial statements to be altered if the amount was material, is the insolvency of a debtor as at the date of the balance sheet which only becomes known after the financial statements have been approved by the board.

Contingencies and Commitments

Company law requires the disclosure in the notes of contingent liabilities and capital commitments.

A contingency is a condition which exists at the balance sheet date, the outcome of which will be confirmed only on the occurrence or non-occurrence of one or more uncertain events. British Vita [p. 25, note 26] has a number of contingent liabilities; it has, for example, guaranteed some of the overdrafts and third party liabilities of certain of its subsidiaries. Standard accounting practice also requires disclosure of contingent assets.

As required by law, British Vita discloses in note 12 [p. 20] its commitments for capital expenditure not provided for in the accounts and capital expenditure authorized by the directors but not contracted for. The reader of the annual report thus has knowledge of important projected cash outlays in the forthcoming period.

3. Taxation and Audit

Taxation?
Wherein? And what taxation? My Lord Cardinal,
You that are blamed alike with us,
Know you of this taxation?
WILLIAM SHAKESPEARE, *King Henry the Eighth*, I.ii

Never ask of money spent
Where the spender thinks it went
Nobody was ever meant
To remember or invent
What he did with every cent
ROBERT FROST, *The Hardship of Accounting*

This short chapter deals briefly with two important matters of which all readers of company reports should have some knowledge: taxation and audit. No attempt will be made to go into either in detail; company taxation in particular can become fearsomely complicated.

Taxation in the Accounts

There are several references to taxation in British Vita's 1985 annual report and accounts. Taxation provided on the group profit for the year ended 31 December 1985 is stated in the profit and loss account to be £5,075,000, that is, 41 per cent of the profit on ordinary activities before taxation of £12,231,000. The current liabilities (creditors: amounts falling due within one year) include corporation tax of £2,857,000 and other taxes and social security costs of £4,073,000. Amounts falling due after more than one year also include corporation tax to the amount of £275,000. The provisions for liabilities and charges include deferred taxation of £497,000. The source and application of funds statement shows taxation paid (£3,193,000) as an application of funds. Further details of the company's tax position are given in note 7 [p. 18].

Corporation Tax

Companies pay corporation tax, not income tax. Taxable income is measured very much in the same way as accounting profit, with the major exception of depreciation. The corporation tax rate is imposed annually in arrears for the financial year 1 April to 31 March. The tax is *assessed*, however, on the basis of a company's accounting period. British Vita's accounting period ends, it will be remembered, on 31 December each year. The tax is payable for most companies nine months after the end of the financial year in which the company's accounting period ends. The rate of corporation tax can vary. In the financial year 1985 (i.e., from 1 April 1985 to 31 March 1986) it was 40 per cent. The lower rate of 30 per cent applied to small profits. In the financial year 1986 the rates were 35 per cent and 29 per cent respectively.

When a dividend is paid by a company it pays advance corporation tax (ACT), an advance payment on the corporation tax liability, to the Inland Revenue. The amount paid depends on the basic rate of income tax. Shareholders are taxed on the dividend grossed up at the basic rate, but receive a tax credit which can be set against their liability to income tax. The example on page 35, which assumes a corporation tax rate of 35 per cent (the rate for the financial year 1986) and a basic rate of income tax of 29 per cent, shows how this 'imputation system', as it is called, works.

The dividends paid or proposed are shown in the company's accounts as the cash amounts received or receivable by the shareholders.

Suppose that the shareholder is a person (male), not a company, and holds all the shares. He would be assessed for income tax on £634, not £450. If he pays tax at 29 per cent, he can set off his tax credit of £184 against his liability to tax of the same amount. If he pays tax at less than 29 per cent, he is entitled to a refund; if he pays at more than 29 per cent, he has more to pay. A shareholder which is a company would treat such a dividend as 'franked investment income' and would not be assessed to

	£000
Taxable profit	1,000
Corporation tax at 35%	350
Profit after tax	650
Dividend paid	450
Retained profit	200
ACT paid by company (29/71 × £450)	184
The shareholders receive:	
dividend	450
plus tax credit	184
	634

corporation tax on it. It could pass on the tax credit to its own shareholders.

The company itself can normally (but not always, see below) recover the ACT paid (£184) by setting it off against its liability to corporation tax (£350) on its taxable profits. The difference (£166) is called 'mainstream' corporation tax.

Capital Allowances and Investment Incentives

As already noted in Chapter 2, capital allowances differ in amount from the depreciation shown in a company's accounts. The main reason for this is that while a company in reporting to its shareholders is interested in calculating profit as accurately as possible, the government may also be interested in trying to encourage investment.

The method of calculating capital allowances has varied from time to time, as have the rates allowed. At the time of writing, most capital allowances are given in the form of annual writing-down allowances calculated on the reducing balance method as illustrated in the depreciation examples in Chapter 2 (p. 20). The rates vary according to the class of asset. There are no capital allowances on non-industrial buildings such as retail shops, offices and dwelling-houses.

It is important to note that all the allowances described above operate as deductions in the calculation of taxable income. If the latter is large enough to cover the allowances, then their effect is to reduce the company's tax bill by the amount of the allowances multiplied by the corporation tax rate. A company which has no taxable income to offset against the allowances does not benefit at all.

This is not true of government grants. These are not reductions in taxable income but payments of cash to a company by the government. They are thus not dependent on the company making a taxable profit. The receipt of such grants does not affect capital allowances. It is standard accounting practice for grants relating to fixed assets to be credited to profit and loss account over the expected useful life of the asset, *either* reducing the cost of the acquisition of the fixed asset by the amount of the grant, *or* by treating the amount of the grant as a deferred credit (shown separately in the balance sheet), a portion of which is transferred to revenue annually. British Vita uses the second method, in 1985 crediting government grants of £120,000 to profit and loss account [p. 17] and carrying forward £600,000 as deferred income [p. 22]. Other grants are credited to revenue in the year in which the expenditure to which they relate is charged.

Deferred Taxation

Capital allowances greater than accounting depreciation are an example of what is known as a 'timing difference'. The effect is to reduce taxable income in the current year below the company's profit before tax.

It could be argued that the taxation payable has not been saved but merely 'deferred' to a later year. Whether, and if so how, a provision should be made for 'deferred taxation' is a matter which has aroused a lot of discussion in the accounting world. British Vita's policy in this matter is set out in its Accounting Policies [p. 15] as follows:

Provision is made for deferred taxation in circumstances where there is a reasonable probability of payment in the foreseeable future. The provision is established at corporation tax rates anticipated to be in force at the time the deferred liability is expected to crystallize. Advance corporation tax which is available to reduce the corporation tax payable on future profits is carried forward and, to the extent appropriate, is deducted from the provision for deferred taxation.

British Vita thus, in accordance with standard accounting practice, makes provision not for all potential future deferred tax payable but only for that part where there is a reasonable probability that payment will have to be made in the foreseeable future (usually regarded as the next three years). Note 7 [p. 18] discloses that 'full' provision for deferred tax would have amounted to £3,139,000, as distinct from the 'partial' provision made at £497,000. The difference in these amounts shows how important it is to know how a company has treated deferred taxation.

In employing corporation tax rates anticipated to be in force at the time the deferred liability is expected to crystallize (namely, 35 per cent), British Vita is using what is known as the 'liability method'.

The provision is smaller than it otherwise would have been by the amount of ACT recoverable deducted. ACT recoverable arises mainly because the ACT which British Vita has to pay on its proposed dividends is payable within the next accounting period (1986), whereas it is recoverable only in 1987. This simultaneously gives rise to a *current* liability and a *deferred* asset. It is the latter which is deducted from the provision for deferred taxation.

Where a company has no liability to corporation tax, the ACT is not recoverable and has to be written off. Such a situation may be caused by a combination of low profitability and generous tax allowances.

Capital Gains Tax

Individuals are taxed not only on their income but also, at a rate of 30 per cent, on certain capital gains, that is, the excess of the price they receive on selling an asset over the price they paid for it. Companies are not liable to capital gains tax on their capital gains, which are instead charged to corporation tax. So that the gain is charged at 30 per cent, a reducing fraction ($\frac{1}{7}$ in 1986) is applied to the corporation tax rate.

Tax does not become payable when an asset is revalued unless it is sold. Since fixed assets are held for use rather than sale, it is not the practice to make provision for the tax which would arise if the assets were sold for the revalued amount (see British Vita's note 7, p. 18).

If a gain is made from selling an asset owned on 6 April 1965, only that part of the gain related to the period from 6 April 1965 to the date of sale is taxable. It is for this reason that some companies include a note in their annual reports giving the market value of their shares at that date. (British Vita does not do so because it was not then a listed company.)

Close Companies

The Finance Act 1965 introduced the concept of the 'close company', defined as a company resident in the United Kingdom which is under the control of five or fewer participators and associates or of participators who are directors. The detailed legislation is extremely complex but has been of little practical importance since 1980. British Vita states in its Directors' Report that it is not a close company [p. 9].

Tax Law

The most important statutes (Acts of Parliament) relating to the taxes described in this chapter are the Finance Acts 1965 and 1972, the Capital Allowances Act 1968, the Income and Corporation Taxes Act 1970 and the Taxes Management Act 1970. Every year there is at least one Finance Act amending the law. There is also a large body of case law relating to taxation. The law is thus always changing and some of the statements made in this chapter will need modification as the years go by.

Audit

The preparation of the financial statements of a company and their presentation to the shareholders and to the tax authorities are the duties of the directors, not of the auditors, although the latter, of course, often give valuable assistance. Since there are often misconceptions about the functions of auditors, it is worth looking carefully at the report they give.

The Report of the Auditors to the members (i.e., shareholders) of British Vita Company Ltd [p. 11] reads as follows:

To the Members of British Vita P L C

We have audited the accounts set out on pages 12 to 27 in accordance with approved Auditing Standards.

In our opinion the accounts, which have been prepared under the historical cost convention as modified by the revaluation of certain fixed assets, give a true and fair view of the state of affairs of the Company and the Group at 31 December 1985 and of the profit and source and application of funds of the Group for the year then ended and comply with the Companies Act 1985.

The report is signed by Arthur Andersen & Co., who are one of the so-called Big Eight international accounting firms. The audits of UK listed companies are increasingly carried out by Big Eight accounting firms.

There are a number of interesting points to note about this report:

1. It is a report, not a certificate or guarantee: the auditors report their opinion; they do not certify or guarantee anything.
2. What they give their opinion on is the 'truth and fairness' of the accounts. This is not the same as saying that the accounts are 'correct' in every particular. It should be clear from the discussion of the financial statements in Chapter 2 that the figures in balance sheets and profit and loss accounts are necessarily based to a certain extent on judgements.
3. The auditors are reporting to the members (shareholders)

of British Vita, not to the directors. Their function, as a late-nineteenth-century English judge put it, is to serve as a 'watchdog' for the shareholders. They are appointed by the shareholders, usually on the recommendation of the directors. Appointment is made each year by resolution at the annual general meeting.
4. No reference is made to the discovery of mistakes or fraud. These are regarded as incidental to the main purpose of reporting as to 'truth and fairness'.

It is obviously important that auditors should not only be skilled in their profession but also be independent of the directors and managers of the company being audited. It is therefore provided by the Companies Act that, firstly, auditors should either be members of a body of accountants established in the United Kingdom and recognized by the Department of Trade and Industry or be authorized by the Department to be appointed, and that, secondly, the auditor must not be an officer or servant of the company or of any company in the group, or a partner or employee of such officer or servant.

The amount of the auditors' remuneration must be stated in the annual report. For the British Vita group in 1985 it was £240,000 [p. 17].

The references in the audit report to the historical cost convention are explained in Chapter 4.

4. Regulation, Formats, Accounting Standards and Inflation

Regulation

In order to draw up a set of financial statements for a company it is necessary to make decisions about:

1. What should be disclosed (*disclosure*).
2. The format of the statements (*presentation*).
3. The rules of measurement and valuation (*valuation*).

Who should make these decisions (that is, how, if at all, should company financial statements be regulated)? There are a number of possibilities:

1. Each company is allowed to decide for itself.
2. The accountancy profession, as acknowledged experts in the field, makes the decisions.
3. The government makes the decisions by means of:
   (i) legislation;
   (ii) a government-controlled regulatory body;
   (iii) a national accounting plan; or
   (iv) an accounting court.

It is possible, of course, that a mixture of the above methods may be appropriate.

Whichever methods are chosen, there are costs and benefits. No one method is likely to be ideal for all countries and at all times. In this chapter we shall look at the British approach in the 1980s. It has to be remembered that it is the result of over a century of evolution and that British ideas on the subject are increasingly being influenced by the United States and by the other member states of the E E C.

During the nineteenth century most British companies were allowed complete freedom in matters of disclosure, presentation and valuation. During the twentieth century it gradually became accepted that, while the government should not interfere with presentation and valuation, it ought to prescribe by legislation what should be disclosed. This was the general philosophy behind the Companies Act 1948. The Act imposed two obligations on company directors: firstly, to prepare balance sheets and profit and loss accounts which gave a 'true and fair view' and, secondly, to give the detailed information specified in a Schedule to the Act. No definition was given of the phrase 'true and fair'.

This approach was commented on favourably in the report of the 1962 committee on company law amendment:

> In our view the general scheme of the Act in this respect is the right one, namely to indicate in general terms the objectives and the standard of disclosure required and also to prescribe certain specific information that must be given. The formula 'true and fair' seems to us satisfactory as an indication of the required standard, while it makes for certainty to prescribe certain specific information which the law regards as the minimum necessary for the purpose of attaining that standard.
> (*Report of the Company Law Committee* (Cmnd. 1749, 1962), para. 332)

The committee went on to state that 'it is primarily to the initiative of the professional associations that we must look if the general principles of the Act are to be effectively applied in practice' (para. 334). They referred in particular to the Recommendations on Accounting Principles issued periodically by the Institute of Chartered Accountants in England and Wales (the 'English Institute'). It was through these Recommendations (issued between 1942 and 1969) that the professional accountancy bodies began to involve themselves in matters of presentation and valuation.

During the 1960s the quality of published financial statements was increasingly criticized. The profession responded in 1970 with the establishment of an Accounting Standards Committee (A S C). The establishment of such a committee was encouraged by the government.

The British government has made no serious attempt to control company financial statements through a regulatory agency (as exists in the United States in the form of the Securities and Exchange Commission), a national accounting plan (as in France) or an accounting court (as in the Netherlands). It has, however, intervened on matters of disclosure and in the debate about inflation accounting (see below) and, as a result of Britain's entry into the E E C, has legislated on presentation and valuation.

In Britain, then, it is company legislation and the accounting standards published by the A S C which largely determine what goes into published financial statements. Less important influences are tax legislation and the requirements of the Stock Exchange. Tax legislation influences published accounts because companies may find it inconvenient to follow one set of practices for tax purposes and another for reporting to shareholders. Accounting practices banned for tax calculations tend to be unpopular in published financial statements, but there is no compulsion for a company to follow tax rules in those statements. (In this respect Britain differs from many continental European countries.)

Stock Exchange requirements for listed companies do not go much beyond those of company law and the accountancy profession. Listed companies are expected to comply with statements of standard accounting practice (see below).

The relevant requirements of the Companies Act 1985 are summarized in the Glossary (Appendix B) under a number of headings, the most important of which are: Debtors, Directors' Emoluments, Directors' Report, Distributable Reserves, Employee Information, Liabilities, Segment Reporting, True and Fair View, Turnover and Undistributable Reserves.

Formats

Companies have a choice of two balance sheet formats and four profit and loss account formats. The minimum requirements of one of the balance sheet formats are illustrated in Table 4.1. The other format is identical except that it is set out horizontally rather than vertically. Headings for which there is no balance may be omitted, and additional detail may be added. British Vita, for example, has omitted the heading Intangible assets and has added the heading Minority interest.

The four profit and loss account formats are more flexible. Two are vertical and two horizontal. Most companies publish a profit and loss account very much like British Vita's, but others disclose the costs of raw materials and consumables, staff costs and depreciation, instead of distribution costs and administrative expenses.

Small and medium companies (defined in terms of total assets, turnover and average number of employees) have the privilege of filing modified accounts with the Registrar of Companies, but the modifications do not apply to the financial statements sent to shareholders. Subsidiaries may take advantage of the modifications only if the group to which they belong is as a whole small or medium. No listed companies are regarded as small or medium.

Accounting Standards

The ASC is at present composed of twenty-one part-time, unpaid members from both the private and public sectors. Appointments to the committee are made by the presidents of the six UK and Irish professional accountancy bodies (namely, the Institute of Chartered Accountants in England and Wales; the Institute of Chartered Accountants of Scotland; the Institute of Chartered Accountants in Ireland; the Chartered Association of Certified Accountants; the Chartered Institute of Management Accountants; and the Chartered Institute of Public Finance and Accountancy). Up to five members are 'users' of the accounts who need not be, but often are, qualified accountants. The

Table 4.1. Balance Sheet Format

	£	£
Fixed assets		
Intangible assets	X	
Tangible assets	X	
Investments	X	
		X
Current assets		
Stocks	X	
Debtors	X	
Investments	X	
Cash at bank and in hand	X	
	X	
Creditors: amounts falling due within one year	(X)	
Net current assets (liabilities)		X
Total assets less current liabilities		XX
Creditors: amounts falling due after more than one year		X
Provisions for liabilities and charges		X
Capital and reserves		
Called-up share capital	X	
Share premium account	X	
Revaluation reserve	X	
Other reserves	X	
Profit and loss account	X	
		X
		XX

Source: Companies Act 1985, Schedule 4.

ASC operates by issuing 'exposure drafts' for comment by interested parties. Later, a definitive statement is issued.

At 31 December 1987, twenty-three Statements of Standard Accounting Practice (SSAPs) had been issued:

1. Accounting for the results of associated companies.
2. Disclosure of accounting policies.
3. Earnings per share.
4. The accounting treatment of government grants.
5. Accounting for value added tax.
6. Extraordinary items and prior year adjustments.
7. Accounting for changes in the purchasing power of money (a provisional standard replaced by SSAP 16).
8. The treatment of taxation under the imputation system in the accounts of companies.
9. Stocks and work in progress.
10. Statements of source and application of funds.
11. Accounting for deferred taxation (replaced by SSAP 15).
12. Accounting for depreciation.
13. Accounting for research and development.
14. Group accounts.
15. Accounting for deferred taxation.
16. Current cost accounting.
17. Accounting for post balance sheet events.
18. Accounting for contingencies.
19. Accounting for investment properties.
20. Foreign currency translation.
21. Accounting for leases and hire purchase contracts.
22. Accounting for goodwill.
23. Accounting for acquisitions and mergers.

It will be noted that SSAPs 7 and 11 have already been replaced by new ones. Not all exposure drafts have become statements of standard accounting practice.

The ASC also approves the issue of non-mandatory Statements of Recommended Practice (SORPs). As at 31 December 1987 two had been issued: one on pension scheme accounts by the ASC itself, and the other on disclosures about oil and gas exploration and production activities issued by the Oil Industry Accounting Committee and 'franked' (approved) by the ASC.

Statements of standard accounting practice are inevitably to some extent 'political' documents. The professional accountancy bodies have no legal right to lay down accounting practices or to say what must be disclosed in company financial statements.

They do, of course, have authority over their own members. Where a company does not observe an accounting standard, it is expected to disclose the fact and to explain its reasons. All significant departures from accounting standards will be referred to in the auditors' report, whether or not they are disclosed in the accounts. If the auditors consider that a departure is not justified, they will qualify their report and, if practicable, they will also quantify the financial effect of the departure. In exceptional circumstances the directors may consider, and the auditors may agree, that a departure is required in order to show a true and fair view. In such a case, the auditors will mention it and their agreement to it but will not qualify their report.

The various statements of standard accounting practice are very important. References to them will be found throughout this book. The most general one is SSAP 2 on the disclosure of accounting policies. This sets out four basic assumptions or concepts which are said to underlie the periodic accounts of business enterprises:

---

1. The 'going concern' concept: the enterprise will continue in operational existence for the foreseeable future.
2. The 'accruals' concept: revenues and costs are accrued (that is, recognized as they are earned or incurred, not as money is received or paid), matched with one another as far as their relationship can be established or justifiably assumed, and dealt with in the profit and loss account of the period to which they relate.
3. The 'consistency' concept: there is consistency of accounting treatment of like items within each accounting period and from one period to the next.
4. The 'prudence' concept: revenue and profits are not anticipated, but are recognized by inclusion in the profit and loss account only when realized in the form either of cash or of other assets the ultimate realization of which can be assessed with reasonable certainty; provision is made for all known liabilities whether the amount of these is known with certainty or is a best estimate in the light of the information available.

Where there is a conflict between the accruals and prudence concepts, the latter usually prevails.

Most accountants would agree that the above concepts are reasonably descriptive of actual practice; not all would accept that these are the concepts which *ought* to be followed. In particular, there are those who think too much stress is laid on prudence, or conservatism as they would prefer to call it.

Concepts not mentioned in SSAP 2 are 'objectivity' and 'substance over form'. Objectivity arises from the need to establish rules for recording financial transactions and events which as far as possible do not depend on the personal judgement of the recorder. This has led to a bias in favour of using the cost of acquisition, or historical cost as it is usually called. A brief description of traditional British accounting practice would be historical cost modified by prudence. Many accountants have denied that it is a function of a balance sheet to show how much a company is worth. It is, they have argued, merely a historical record. Other accountants have argued, however, that a balance sheet which did not attempt to show how much a company is worth would be of little use to the shareholders.

'Substance over form' is a concept whereby transactions or other events are accounted for and presented in accordance with their economic reality rather than their legal form. It is particularly applicable to borrowings which are not legally debt and therefore might be shown 'off balance sheet' but which have the same economic function as debt. Finance leases (see Chapter 8), for example, fall into this category.

As a result of SSAP 2, companies publish statements of 'accounting policies' setting out the way in which they have dealt with a number of matters. British Vita's statement, for example [p. 15], covers the basis of the accounts (that is, the historical cost convention modified to include the revaluation of certain fixed assets), the basis of consolidation, foreign currency balances, turnover, depreciation of tangible fixed assets, stocks, grants, research and development, patents and trade marks, pensions and taxation.

Accounting for Inflation

During the last two decades changes in both general and specific

Table 4.2. Inflation Rates, 1971–86

	Index (average for calendar year)	Percentage increase over the previous year
1971	80·0	—
1972	85·7	7·1
1973	93·5	9·1
1974	108·5	16·0
1975	134·8	24·2
1976	157·1	16·5
1977	182·0	15·8
1978	197·1	8·3
1979	223·5	13·4
1980	263·7	18·0
1981	295·0	11·9
1982	320·4	8·6
1983	335·1	4·6
1984	351·8	5·0
1985	373·2	6·1
1986	385·9	3·4

Source: Index of Retail Prices (1 January 1974 = 100) as reported in *Accountancy*.

Table 4.3. The Rate of Exchange of £1 to US$1, 1971–86

31 December		
	1971	2·55
	1972	2·35
	1973	2·32
	1974	2·35
	1975	2·02
	1976	1·70
	1977	1·91
	1978	2·03
	1979	2·22
	1980	2·38
	1981	1·91
	1982	1·62
	1983	1·45
	1984	1·16
	1985	1·45
	1986	1·47

Source: *UN Monthly Bulletin of Statistics*.

prices and fluctuating exchange rates have caused many problems for accountants. Table 4.2 shows the fall in the domestic purchasing power of the 'pound in the pocket'. Table 4.3 shows the fluctuations of the pound sterling in relation to the United States dollar, the world's major currency.

The Companies Act distinguishes between 'historical cost accounting rules', which require the application to financial statements of conventional accounting procedures based on historical cost modified by prudence, and 'alternative accounting rules', which permit not only the use of current cost valuations but also a mixture of historical and alternative valuations. British Vita, like many other companies, prepares its financial statements 'under the historical cost convention modified to include the revaluation of certain fixed assets' [p. 15].

In times of inflation, balance sheet values based on historical cost rapidly become divorced from current market values, and objectivity and prudence can lead paradoxically to an overstatement of profits. This is most easily understood in relation to fixed assets and depreciation. If fixed assets are valued at historical cost, depreciation will usually be based on historical cost as well. This will result in a lower depreciation charge, and hence a higher profit, than if both the asset and the depreciation were written up to, say, current replacement cost. It can be strongly argued that the use of historical costs during a period of inflation can lead to the publication of profit figures which are in part fictitious. The distribution of such profits would mean a running down of the *real* (as opposed to the money) capital of the company.

The attempts by the leaders of the accountancy profession to introduce some form of inflation accounting have been beset by many difficulties.*

Two principal methods of accounting for inflation have been debated:

1. Adjustments for changes in the *general* price level only, that is, current purchasing power (CPP) accounting.
2. Adjustments for changes in *specific* prices, that is current cost accounting (CCA).

* For a lively account by a participant, see C. A. Westwick, 'The Lessons to be Learned from the Development of Inflation Accounting in the UK', *Accounting and Business Research*, Autumn 1980.

The two methods differ in their approach to profit measurement and asset valuation. CPP accounting values assets in terms of the current purchasing power of the sums of money originally invested. While under historical cost accounting no profit is deemed to be earned unless the original money capital invested is maintained intact, under CPP accounting it is the purchasing power of that capital that has to be maintained. In practice, CPP accounting means that non-monetary assets (that is, fixed assets and stocks) are valued at historical cost adjusted by a general price index. All profit and loss account items are restated by the same index. In addition, profit is decreased or increased by a purchasing power loss or gain calculated on the company's net monetary assets during the period.

CCA accounting, on the other hand, values assets at their 'value to the business', that is, the lower of current replacement cost and 'recoverable amount', the latter being the higher of an asset's net realizable value and the amount recoverable from its further use in the business. In the profit and loss account, current revenues are matched with current costs and no profit is deemed to be earned unless the company has maintained its physical capacity. In practice, CCA profit is calculated by making four adjustments to historical cost operating profit. The adjustments are:

---

1. A cost of sales adjustment (COSA).
2. A monetary working capital adjustment (MWCA).
3. A depreciation adjustment.
4. A gearing adjustment.

The adjustments are applied in two stages:

---

1. To arrive at the *current cost operating profit*. This is equal to the historical cost operating profit after deduction of the first three adjustments. It represents the surplus arising from the ordinary activities of the business, after allowing for the impact of price changes on the funds needed to continue the existing business and to maintain its operating capability, but without taking into account the way in which it is financed. It is calculated before interest and after taxation.

2. To arrive at the *current cost profit attributable to share-holders.* This is the current cost operating profit after deduction of the gearing adjustment. It represents the surplus for the period after allowing for the impact of price changes on the funds needed to maintain the shareholders' proportion of the operating capabilities of the group.

The cost of sales adjustment is made in order to base the cost of sales on the cost current at the time of consumption instead of the time of purchase. This can be done in various ways – for example, by the use of appropriate specific price indices and the so-called averaging method (that is, the adjustment is equal to the average *physical* stock multiplied by the price increase during the year).

Increased prices tie up in the business not only more stocks but also more monetary working capital (that is, in essence, bank balances + debtors − creditors). The MWCA can be calculated by the averaging method in a similar way to the COSA. The depreciation adjustment is made in order to base depreciation on current replacement cost instead of historical cost.

The gearing adjustment is the most controversial. It is intended to indicate the benefit to shareholders of the use of long-term debt, measured by the extent to which the net operating assets are financed by borrowing. In effect, as calculated in SSAP 16, it reduces the three current cost adjustments by the proportion which has been financed by borrowing. The concept of 'gearing' is discussed further in Chapter 8.

The ASC originally preferred CPP accounting, and this was the basis of the provisional SSAP 7 issued in 1974. The government-appointed Sandilands Committee, however, which reported in 1975, rejected CPP accounting in favour of CCA. The standard finally accepted in 1980, SSAP 16, was CCA based. However, lower rates of inflation and controversy about the details of the standard made SSAP 16 difficult to enforce, and it is no longer mandatory. Like many companies, British Vita provides no CCA data in its 1985 annual report.

Accounting for Foreign Exchange

British Vita's subsidiaries and associated companies outside the UK naturally keep their accounts in the appropriate local currency. These foreign financial statements are translated using year-end rates of exchange, that is, by the 'closing rate' method. This is the method that standard accounting practice requires for subsidiaries which operate as separate or quasi-independent entities.

If the rates at the end of the period differ from those obtaining at the beginning of the year, an exchange or translation difference will arise. Under the closing rate method such gains or losses are dealt with through reserves and do not pass through the profit and loss account. Moreover, any gains or losses arising from borrowings in foreign currency made in order to finance these foreign investments can be netted off against the exchange differences. In a world of sharply fluctuating exchange rates, exchange differences can be quite large, as is demonstrated by British Vita's note 23 [p. 24].

An alternative method of foreign currency translation is the so-called 'temporal method', which is used where the operations of the foreign entity are regarded as an integral part of those of the parent company. The temporal method differs from the closing rate method in that those assets recorded in the local currency at historical cost rather than at a current value (that is, fixed assets and most stocks) are translated at the rates ruling at the dates of acquisition. Also, and very importantly, exchange gains and losses are passed through the profit and loss account. Under the temporal method, groups whose parent company's currency is strengthening tend to show translation gains, while those whose parent company's currency is weakening tend to show translation losses.

For foreign entities whose economies are experiencing very high rates of inflation, British standard accounting practice requires restatement of the financial statement to take account of inflation before application of the closing rate method.

5. Tools of Analysis and Sources of Information

. . . high Heaven rejects the lore
Of nicely-calculated less or more
WILLIAM WORDSWORTH, *Inside of King's College Chapel, Cambridge*

The first four chapters of this book have been mainly descriptive. In the chapters which follow we turn to analysis and interpretation. We shall be concerned with three main questions:

1. Is the company under analysis making a satisfactory profit?
2. Is the company likely to run out of cash, or to keep cash idle?
3. How does the company decide the sources of its long-term funds?

These are the related problems of profitability, liquidity and capital structure.

Our tools of analysis will be the relationships which exist among the different items in the financial statements ('financial ratios') and the rates of return linking outflows with expected inflows ('yields').

Financial Ratios

Financial ratios are normally expressed either as percentages or by the number of times one figure can be divided into another. For example, if a company has current assets of £10,000 and current liabilities of £5,000, we could say that current liabilities are 50 per cent of current assets, that current assets are 200 per cent of current liabilities, that the ratio $\dfrac{\text{current assets}}{\text{current liabilities}}$ is 2.0, or that the ratio $\dfrac{\text{current liabilities}}{\text{current assets}}$ is 0.5. Which method is chosen is a matter of convenience and convention. In the example quoted it is customary to speak of a current ratio, $\dfrac{\text{current assets}}{\text{current liabilities}}$, of 2.0. (A percentage, as can be seen from the above, is merely a ratio multiplied by 100.)

Not all ratios and percentages are significant or useful, and one must guard against the temptation to calculate them for their own sake. The component parts of a ratio must be reasonably related to each other and measure something important. It is unlikely, for example, that much can be gained from a scrutiny of the relationship between current liabilities and goodwill. The limitations of conventional historical cost accounting must always be kept in mind, and accounting figures should not be treated as more precise than they really are. There is little sense in calculating a ratio to more than two decimal places.

A single ratio in isolation seldom provides much information. Each ratio calculated should either confirm what has already been deduced or act as a guide to the further questions which need to be asked.

Yields

A yield is a rate of return relating outflows to inflows. If, for example, I buy for £50 an irredeemable government bond with a par value of £100 on which interest of 4 per cent is payable annually, there is an immediate cash outflow of £50, followed by a series of cash inflows of £4 each year in perpetuity. The yield (gross of tax) is $\dfrac{4 \times 100}{50}\%$, (i.e., 8 per cent). If the bond were redeemable at a fixed price at some date in the future, there would be a difference between the flat yield, which takes only the interest into account, and the redemption yield, which takes the redemption price into account as well. For example, if the bond is redeemable twenty years hence at par, the flat yield is about 5·0 per cent and the redemption yield about 9·8 per cent. Yields such as these can be calculated using compound interest tables, specially compiled bond tables or a suitable computer program.

The Need for Comparisons

As already noted, any ratio, percentage or yield is of little value in isolation. It is necessary to have some standard with which to compare it. The standard can be a budgeted one, set by the company for itself; a historical one, based on the past performance of the company; or an industry one, based on the observed ratios of companies in the same industry.

Budgeted standards are not usually available to shareholders or external financial analysts. Historical comparisons are often given in annual reports: see, for example, page 10 of British Vita's report, headed 'British Vita Group 1981–1985'.

Industry Ratios

Industry ratios pose a much more difficult problem to the financial analyst. There are a number of reasons for this.

Firstly, it is often difficult to decide to which industry a company belongs. Many industries are, in fact, composed of a surprisingly heterogeneous group of companies. In the Stock Exchange industrial classification British Vita is included in the plastics and rubber fabricators' group, which includes nine other companies. British Vita is the largest of the ten companies, with almost half of the total industry turnover. It is the only company in the industry with substantial overseas sales. (The standard industrial classification used in government publications is not identical with the Stock Exchange classification. In this book we shall follow the custom of most financial analysts in using the latter.)

Secondly, the emphasis of the system of accounting at present in use is on *consistency* for a particular company over time, rather than *comparability* among different companies at a single point in time, and the analyst must constantly be on his guard against differences in definition and in methods of valuation.

Thirdly, companies end their accounting periods on different dates, so that industry ratios are perforce averages of ratios calculated at different dates and for different periods.

For these reasons not too much reliance can be placed on an industry comparison which is based on ratios obtained from published accounts. Companies can, however, obtain comparable ratios by taking part in a properly conducted comparison, such as those conducted by the Centre for Interfirm Comparison.* But such ratios are, by their very nature, confidential and unavailable to the external analyst.

Sources of Information

In this section are listed a number of useful sources of information relating to individual companies, to industries or to the company sector as a whole. The list is not intended to be exhaustive. Most of the items should be available in a good public or university library. The Central Statistical Office publishes each year a brief, up-to-date guide to government statistics (*Government Statistics: A Brief Guide to Sources*). There is also a more comprehensive *Guide to Official Statistics*.

1. *The Times 1000* (published annually by *The Times*). This lists each year, among other things, the thousand largest British industrial companies, with details of their turnover; capital employed (defined as total tangible assets less current liabilities, other than bank loans and overdrafts and future tax); net profit before interest and tax; net profit before interest and tax as a percentage of turnover; net profit before interest and tax as a percentage of capital employed; number of employees; and the market capitalization of the equity (that is, the total market value of all the company's ordinary shares). British Vita is in the top five hundred of the thousand.

2. *Company Finance* (available annually by subscription from HMSO; it is MA3 in the 'Business Monitor' series). It contains tables showing for both listed and for non-listed companies, and by industrial sector:

* See H. Ingham and L. T. Harrington, *Interfirm Comparison* (Heinemann, 1980).

1. A balance sheet summary.
2. Income and appropriation account.
3. Sources and uses of funds.
4. Various accounting ratios.
5. Size distributions.

3. *Financial Statistics* (published monthly by the Central Statistical Office; an 'explanatory handbook' is published annually). Section 8 gives balance sheet, profit and loss account and funds statement data for industrial and commercial companies as a whole. More up to date than *Company Finance.*

4. *British Business* (published weekly by the Department of Trade and Industry).

5. *Economic Trends* (published monthly by HMSO).

6. *Bank of England Quarterly Bulletin.*

7. *UK National Accounts* (the 'CSO Blue Book'; published annually by HMSO.) Statistics on the company sector are published from time to time in numbers 4 to 7. The first three also carry useful articles interpreting the statistics.

8. *Quality of Markets Quarterly* (published by the Stock Exchange).

9. *Stock Exchange Press Company Handbook* (published bi-annually by the Stock Exchange).

10. *The Stock Exchange Official Year-Book* (published annually by the Stock Exchange).

These last three publications provide a wealth of information on all aspects of the British stock market.

11. *Financial Reporting. A Survey of Published Accounts* (published annually by The Institute of Chartered Accountants in England and Wales). This is a guide to current accounting requirements and an analysis of methods and examples of financial reporting used by 300 major British industrial and commercial companies.

12. *Accounting Standards* (published annually by the Institute of Chartered Accountants in England and Wales). This contains the full texts of all UK exposure drafts and accounting standards

extant at 1 May each year. Also contains background material on the Accounting Standards Committee.

13. *Current Accounting Law and Practice* (published annually by Sweet & Maxwell). This reproduces all relevant statute law, case law and accounting standards.

14. *Price Index Numbers for Current Cost Accounting* (published monthly by the Department of Trade and Industry). This provides essential data for the preparation of current cost accounts.

15. *Sources of British Business Comparative Performance Data* (2nd ed. 1986, no. 193 in the Accountants Digest Series published by The Institute of Chartered Accountants in England and Wales).

16. *MicroEXSTAT Database.* This contains regularly updated data extracted from the annual reports and accounts of over 2,300 UK commercial and industrial companies, including all companies trading on the Stock Exchange and the Unlisted Securities Market, all private companies included in *The Times 1000*, and all UK subsidiaries of international companies in *The Times 1000*. A maximum of six years' data is provided for each company. Industry data are also provided, based on the Stock Exchange classification.

Access to the *MicroEXSTAT Database* is by microcomputer. Full details are available from Extel Statistical Services Ltd, 37–45 Paul St, London EC2A 4PB.

6. Profitability, Return on Investment and Value Added

For what is Worth in anything
But so much Money as 'twill bring
SAMUEL BUTLER, *Hudibras*, I,i

Profitability

One of the first questions a shareholder is likely to ask of his company is whether it is making a profit. If so, is it making a satisfactory profit? We have already encountered some of the difficulties which arise in trying to measure profit. Although accountants try to make measurements as objective as possible, many financial numbers, even those purporting to represent past events, are necessarily to some extent estimates. Profit is especially affected by the difficulties of measuring depreciation and valuing stock-in-trade, difficulties which are accentuated in times of changing price levels.

In this chapter we shall look at the British Vita group's profit record for the years 1983 to 1985.

Return on Investment

Sales (turnover) and profits cannot be looked at in isolation from the investment in net assets made to achieve them. The relationship between them can be set out as follows:

$$\text{Return on investment (ROI)} = \frac{\text{profit}}{\text{net assets}} = \frac{\text{profit}}{\text{sales}} \times \frac{\text{sales}}{\text{net assets}}$$

As already noted, there are a number of 'profit' figures in British Vita's consolidated profit and loss account, namely, gross profit, operating profit, profit on ordinary activities before taxation, profit on ordinary activities after taxation, profit before extraordinary items and profit for the year. Only two profit measures are suitable for use in the present context. They are (a) operating profit and (b) profit on ordinary activities before taxation and interest (which is equal to operating profit plus share of profit of associated companies). The strength of these measures is that, while taking account (as gross profit does not) of most of the revenues and expenses, they are not affected by interest on loans, dividends on shares, taxation or extraordinary items. If return on investment is to be a satisfactory measure of managerial performance on a continuing basis, it should not be influenced by changes in financial structure (see Chapter 8) or by changes in rates of tax. Similarly, it should not be affected by items which are not expected to recur frequently or regularly. The advantage of (a) over (b) is that it produces a return on investment measure which is easier to decompose since it does not include the profits of associated companies and can therefore be compared with turnover figures which, as we have seen (p. 26), do not include sales made by such companies.

If profit is defined as operating profit or profit before taxation and interest, net assets must be defined consistently as assets net of current liabilities but not of longer-term liabilities. This is equal to capital employed as shown on the face of British Vita's balance sheets.

In principle, return on investment can be measured in either historical cost or current cost terms. In practice, most companies (British Vita among them) provide only historical cost data, although these are often modified by the revaluation of land and buildings.

British Vita on page 10 of its 1985 annual report discloses for the years 1981 to 1985 both profit on ordinary activities before taxation and interest as a percentage of *average* capital employed and also operating profit as a percentage of the turnover of the company and its subsidiaries (but not its associated companies).

Table 6.1. Calculation of Historical Cost Return on Investment, British Vita Group, 1982–5

	Operating profit (a) £000	Share of profit of associated companies (b) £000	Profit on ordinary activities before taxation and interest (c) = (a) + (b) £000	Capital employed (d) £000	Average capital employed (e)* £000	Profit on ordinary activities before taxation and interest as a percentage of average capital employed (f) = (c)/(e) × 100 %
1982	5,063	3,447	8,510	48,830	47,830	17·8
1983	7,947	3,520	11,467	51,105	50,467	22·7
1984	9,528	3,884	13,412	61,745	56,925	23·6
1984†	7,824	3,884	11,708	61,493	56,799	20·6
1985	11,790	2,584	14,374	63,370	62,431	23·0

* Average capital employed for 1985 is equal to the average of capital employed 1984 and capital employed 1985, and similarly for other years.
† Restated.
Source: British Vita PLC, *Annual Report and Accounts 1985*, page 10.

Table 6.2. Calculation of Historical Cost Operating Profit as Percentage of Turnover, British Vita Group, 1982–5

	Turnover (a) £000	Operating profit (b) £000	Operating profit as a percentage of turnover (c) = (b)/(a) × 100 %
1982	97,799	5,063	5·2
1983	109,677	7,947	7·2
1984	138,391	9,528	6·9
1984*	133,950	7,824	5·8
1985	186,108	11,790	6·3

* Restated.
Source: ibid.

The details of the calculations for 1982 to 1985 are set out in Tables 6.1 and 6.2.

The tables show that in historical cost terms turnover nearly doubled between 1982 and 1985, but that both operating profit as a percentage of turnover and return on investment were relatively stable. The 1984 restatement, which arises from the effective exclusion of the group's Zambian operations from the consolidated financial statements, has little relative effect on turnover but a significant effect on operating profit. Figures given in the Notes to the Accounts [p. 16] show that the group's Zambian operations are very profitable (profit on ordinary activities as a percentage of turnover was 32 per cent in both 1984 and 1985), but the assets they produce cannot be remitted to the UK without substantial loss.

Analysing the Profit and Loss Account

The detail provided in the consolidated profit and loss and the notes thereto provides opportunities for further analysis. Table 6.3 sets out turnover, each category of expense and each profit measure for the years 1983 to 1985. The meaning of figures in this 'raw' state are, however, rather difficult to grasp. Table 6.4 therefore expresses all the figures as percentages of turnover and

Table 6.3. Turnover, Expenses and Profits, British Vita Group, 1983–5

Year ended 31 December	1983 £000	1984 £000	1984 (restated) £000	1985 £000
Turnover:				
UK	79,263	89,613	89,613	100,833
Europe	20,684	38,430	38,430	78,178
Africa	7,586	7,503	3,062	3,523
Rest of world	2,144	2,845	2,845	3,574
	109,677	138,391	133,950	186,108
Cost of sales	(83,102)	(105,987)	(104,137)	(144,144)
Gross profit	26,575	32,404	29,813	41,964
Distribution costs	6,446	8,061	7,766	10,434
Administration expenses	12,182	14,815	14,223	19,740
	18,628	22,876	21,989	30,174
Operating profit	7,947	9,528	7,824	11,790
Share of profit of associated companies	3,520	3,884	3,884	2,584
Interest (net)	(891)	(1,561)	(1,260)	(2,143)
UK & Europe	5,032	5,943	6,061	9,202
Rest of world	5,544	5,908	4,387	3,029
Profit on ordinary activities before taxation	10,576	11,851	10,448	12,231
Taxation	(3,876)	(4,415)	(3,731)	(5,075)
Profit on ordinary activities after taxation	6,700	7,436	6,717	7,156
Minority interests	(123)	(134)	(92)	(70)
Profit before extraordinary items	6,577	7,302	6,625	7,086
Extraordinary items (net of tax)	(413)	(939)	(939)	(3,369)
Profit for the year	6,159	6,363	5,686	3,717

Source: British Vita PLC, *Annual Report and Accounts*, 1984 and 1985.

Table 6.4. Turnover, Expenses and Profits, British Vita Group, 1983–5 (Turnover of Each Year = 100)

Year ended 31 December	1983 %	1984 %	1984 (restated) %	1985 %
Turnover:				
UK	72	65	67	54
Europe	19	28	29	42
Africa	7	5	2	2
Rest of world	2	2	2	2
	100	100	100	100
Cost of sales	(76)	(77)	(78)	(77)
Gross profit	24	23	22	23
Distribution costs	6	6	6	6
Administration expenses	11	11	11	11
	17	17	16	16
Operating profit	7	7	6	6
Share of profit of associated companies	3	3	3	1
Interest (net)	(1)	(1)	(1)	(1)
UK & Europe	4.6	4.3	4.5	4.9
Rest of world	5.1	4.2	3.3	1.6
Profit on ordinary activities before taxation	10	9	8	7
Taxation	(4)	(3)	(3)	(3)
Profit on ordinary activities after taxation	6	5	5	4
Minority interests	0	0	0	0
Profit before extraordinary items	6	5	5	4
Extraordinary items (net of tax)	0	(1)	(1)	(2)
Profit for the year	6	5	4	2

Note: Figures may not add up to totals because of rounding.
Source: ibid.

Table 6.5. Growth Rates, British Vita Group, 1983–5

	1983 %	1984 %	1985 %
Turnover:			
company & subsidiaries	12·1	26·2	38·9
UK		13·1	12·5
Europe		85·8	103·4
Africa		(1·1)	15·1
Rest of World		32·7	25·6
associated companies	3·5	19·5	(15·8)
Operating profit	57·0	19·9	50·7
Share of profit of associated companies	2·1	10·3	(33·5)
Profit on ordinary activities before taxation	43·2	12·1	17·1
UK & Europe		18·1	51·8
Rest of world		6·6	(31·0)
Profit for the year	88·3	3·3	(34.6)

Note: Percentages show percentage increase (decrease) over the previous year
(1983 on 1982; 1984 on 1983; 1985 on 1984 restated).
Source: op. cit., 1983, 1984 and 1985.

Table 6.5 shows the way in which each major item – turnover,
operating profit, share of profit of associated companies, profit
on ordinary activities before interest and tax, and capital employed – have grown since 1983. Turnover is divided into that of
the company and its subsidiaries (the figure used in the previous
tables) and that of the associated companies.

A study of the three tables suggests that, while there has been
little change in the relationship of cost of sales, gross profit,
distribution costs, administrative expenses and operating profit
to turnover, there have been important changes in the geographical composition of turnover and in the relative contribution to
profit of subsidiaries and associated companies. Profit on ordinary activities before taxation has grown each year, but profit for
the year in 1985 was adversely affected by the extraordinary
items (which included closure and restructuring costs and the
loss on the realization of assets blocked in Zambia). The increase
in European turnover and profits is commented on by the chairman in his review as meaning that an increasing percentage of
profits is arising in countries where dividends can be remitted to
the UK without being subject to exchange control restrictions.

		£000
Turnover[1]		186,108
Bought-in materials and services[2]		129,457
Value added (gross)		56,651
Investment income[3]		266
Share of profit of associated companies[1]		2,584
Extraordinary items (gross)[4]		(3,939)
Value added available		55,562
Applied as follows:		
To employees[5]		40,131
To providers of capital:		
interest[6]	2,409	
dividends to British Vita shareholders[1]	2,116	
minority share[1]	70	
		4,595
To governments as taxation[7]		4,385
To retentions for replacement and expansion:		
depreciation[8]	4,850	
retained profit[1]	1,601	
		6,451
		55,562

1. As in the consolidated profit and loss account [p. 12].
2. Balancing figure equal to

Cost of sales		144,144
Distribution costs		10,434
Administrative expenses		19,740
		174,318
less Employment costs [p. 19]	40,131	
Depreciation [p. 17]	4,850	
		44,981
		129,337
add Government grants [p. 17]		120
		129,457

3. Interest received [p. 17].
4. As in consolidated profit and loss account [p. 12], but with taxation added back [p. 18].
5. Employment costs [p. 19].
6. Interest paid [p. 17].
7. Taxation in consolidated profit and loss account (£000)

Taxation in consolidated profit and loss account (£000)	5,075
less taxation on extraordinary items [p. 18]	(570)
less government grants received [p. 17]	(120)
	4,385

8. As disclosed on [p. 17].

This trend is connected with the relative decline in importance of the group's associated companies, since most of these are outside the UK and Europe.

Constructing a Value Added Statement

Technically, a statement of value added is merely another way of displaying the figures for a year's operations but with the emphasis on gross value added (that is, turnover *less* bought-in materials and services) instead of profit. British Vita's for 1985 can be constructed as on page 67. The notes explain where the figures come from.

Analysing the Value Added Statement

A number of useful ratios can be calculated from a value added statement. The ratio of value added to turnover, for example, provides a measure of vertical integration – that is, of the extent to which a group of companies produces its own raw materials and distributes its own products as distinct from buying these from outside. The higher the ratio, the greater the extent of vertical integration. British Vita's ratio (56,651 ÷ 186,108 × 100 = 30 per cent) is relatively low. Value added per £1 of employment costs is £1.41 (£56,651 ÷ 40,131) and value added per employee is £14.14 (56,651 ÷ 4,006). (In making this calculation the employees of the associated companies are excluded: [note 11, page 19].) The more technically advanced an industry, the higher these figures are likely to be. We have already looked in Chapter 2 (p. 14) at the way, expressed in percentage terms, in which the value added is allocated among employees, providers of capital, taxation and retentions.

7. Liquidity and Cash Flows

One may not doubt that, somehow, good
Shall come of water and of mud;
And, sure, the reverent eye must see
A purpose in liquidity
RUPERT BROOKE, *Heaven*

Liquidity

It is very important that a company should be profitable; it is just as important that it should be liquid. We have already seen (pp. 13–15) that an increase in profits must by definition lead to an increase in a company's net assets. There is no reason, however, why its liquid assets, such as cash in the bank, should automatically increase. A profitable and fast-expanding company may in fact find that it has tied up so much of its profits in fixed assets, stocks and debtors that it has difficulty in paying its debts as they fall due. To help prevent such a situation developing a company should prepare a cash budget – that is, a plan of future cash receipts and payments, based on specified assumptions about such things as sales growth, credit terms, issues of shares and expansion of plant. A simplified example demonstrating how a profitable company may run into liquidity problems is given below.

Oodnadatta Ltd is formed on 1 January 1988 to make boomerangs at a cost of £1.50 each and sell them for £2 each. All bills are paid immediately and debts are collected within thirty days. The stock of boomerangs manufactured and paid for in January, for example, will be sold in February and the cash proceeds collected in March. The company's provisional plans are to sell 400 boomerangs in February 1988, 600 in March, 800 in April and so on. At 1 January the company has £600 in cash (raised by

Table 7.1. Oodnadatta Ltd, Cash Budget and Budgeted Profit and Loss Statement, 1988

Budgeted Profit and Loss Statement

	Jan. £	Feb. £	Mar. £	Apr. £	May £	June £	July £	Aug. £	Sep. £	Oct. £	Nov. £	Dec. £	Total £
Sales	—	800	1,200	1,600	2,000	2,400	2,800	3,200	3,600	4,000	4,400	4,800	30,800
Cost of sales	—	600	900	1,200	1,500	1,800	2,100	2,400	2,700	3,000	3,300	3,600	23,100
Profit	—	200	300	400	500	600	700	800	900	1,000	1,100	1,200	7,700

Note: The sales figures are equal to the quantity sold multiplied by £2; the cost of sales figures to the quantity sold multiplied by £1.50; the profit figures to the quantity sold multiplied by £0.50. Note that the cost of sale figures give the cost of the goods *sold* during the month, *not* the cost of the goods *manufactured* during the month.

Cash Budget

	Jan. £	Feb. £	Mar. £	Apr. £	May £	June £	July £	Aug. £	Sep. £	Oct. £	Nov. £	Dec. £
Balance at beginning of month	+600	—	— 900	−1,300	−1,600	−1,800	−1,900	−1,900	−1,800	−1,600	−1,300	− 900
Cash received from debtors	—	+ 800	+1,200	+1,600	+2,000	+2,400	+2,800	+3,200	+3,600	+4,000	+4,400	+4,400
Cash payments to creditors	+600 −600	— 100 −900	− 100 −1,200	−1,500	−1,800	−2,100	−2,400	−2,700	−3,000	−3,300	−3,600	−3,900
Balance at end of month	—	− 900	−1,300	−1,600	−1,800	−1,900	−1,900	−1,800	−1,600	−1,300	− 900	− 400

Note: Cash received from debtors is equal to the sales of the previous month; cash payments to creditors to the cost of sales of the next month.

Table 7.2. Oodnadatta Ltd, Balance Sheets, 1 January and 31 December 1988

Balance Sheets	1 Jan. 1988 £	31 Dec. 1988 £	Difference £
Cash	+ 600	− 400	− 1,000
Debtors	—	+ 4,800	+ 4,800
Stocks	—	+ 3,900	+ 3,900
	+ 600	+ 8,300	+ 7,700
Share capital	+ 600	+ 600	—
Retained profits	—	+ 7,700	+ 7,700
	+ 600	+ 8,300	+ 7,700

Note: The cash figure at 31 December is taken from the cash budget; the debtors represent the December sales, the cash for which will not be collected until January; the stocks represent the cost of goods manufactured and paid for in December for sale in January 1989.

an issue of shares) – just sufficient to cover the manufacture of the first 400 boomerangs – but no other assets.

Before actually starting production, the company draws up monthly budgets relating to profits and cash resources (Table 7.1).

The figures show that although the planned profit for the year is £7,700, cash will fall by £1,000 from a positive £600 to a negative £400. There is thus £8,700 to be accounted for. We can see what will happen by comparing the balance sheet at 1 January with that which will result at 31 December (Table 7.2).

The difference column, which is in fact a simple funds statement, shows the position quite clearly. All the profits, plus the original cash (£600), plus another £400 are tied up in debtors and stocks. It is interesting to note, however, that by the end of January 1989 the company's liquidity crisis will be over:

	Jan. 1989
Balance at beginning of month	− 400
Cash received from debtors	+ 4,800
	+ 4,400
Cash payments to creditors	− 4,200
	£ + 200

The catch is, of course, that, as a result of its 'overtrading', the company is unlikely to reach January 1989, in spite of its excellent profit-making potential, unless it can raise more cash by borrowing, by collecting its debts faster or by keeping down the size of its stocks.

If sales continue to rise similarly in 1989 and costs also remain the same, the company will run into the opposite problem: excess liquidity. The purpose of drawing up cash budgets is to ensure that a company neither runs out of cash nor keeps cash idle when it could be profitably invested.

Current and Liquid Ratios

Although cash budgets are thus an essential part of internal company financial management, they are unavailable to the external financial analyst, who must therefore use rather less precise measures of liquidity. What he tries to do is to approximate the possible future cash flows as closely as possible. It will be remembered that current assets and current liabilities were defined in Chapter 2 as those assets and liabilities which can reasonably be expected to take the form of cash within one year from the date of the balance sheet. One crude measure of liquidity, therefore, is the relationship between the current assets and current liabilities. This is known as the 'current ratio', and is defined as follows:

$$\text{current ratio} = \frac{\text{current assets}}{\text{current liabilities}}$$

In calculating both current assets and current liabilities, care must be taken to exclude any amounts falling due after more than one year. Current ratios can be calculated including or excluding short-term loans (including bank overdrafts and medium- and long-term loans which have reached their final year before repayment). The calculations for the British Vita group are explained in Table 7.3.

Table 7.3. Calculation of Current Ratios, British Vita Group, 1983–5

	Current assets as reported in balance sheet (a) £000	Current assets excluding debtors falling due after more than one year (b) £000	Current liabilities as reported in balance sheet (c) £000	Current liabilities excluding short-term loans (d) £000	Current ratio (e) = (b) ÷ (c)	Current ratio excluding short-term loans (f) = (b) ÷ (d)
1983	44,093	43,638	28,952	25,716	1·51	1·70
1984	61,796	59,539	49,955	37,201	1·19	1·60
1985	74,801	73,192	64,854	53,802	1·13	1·36

Source: British Vita Report and Accounts, 1984 and 1985.

Table 7.4. Calculation of Liquid Ratios, British Vita Group, 1983–5

	Liquid assets (= col. (b) Table 7.3 less stocks and amounts owed by associated companies) (g) £000	Col. (c) Table 7.3 less amounts owing to associated companies (h) £000	Col. (d) Table 7.3 less amounts owing to associated companies (i) £000	Liquid ratio (j) = (g) ÷ (h)	Liquid ratio excluding short-term loans (k) = (g) ÷ (i)
1983	27,262	28,928	25,692	0·94	1·06
1984	37,510*	49,891	37,137	0·75	1·01
1985	50,334	64,854	53,802	0·78	0·94

* Also excludes cash at Zambian banks awaiting remittance approval.
Source: ibid.

A more immediate measure of liquidity can be found by excluding stocks from the numerator. The resulting ratio is known as the liquid, quick or acid-test ratio:

$$\text{liquid ratio} = \frac{\text{current assets} - \text{stocks}}{\text{current liabilities}}$$

The liquid ratio has the incidental advantage of being more easily compared among companies, since it does not depend, as

Table 7.5. Comparison of Current Ratios, 1983–5

	Current ratios		Current ratios excluding short-term loans	
	British Vita group	Industry	British Vita group	Industry
1983	1·51	1·44	1·70	1·86
1984	1·19	1·35	1·60	1·62
1985	1·13	1·30	1·36	1·68

Source: British Vita figures from Table 7.3; Industry figures from MicroEXSTAT.

Table 7.6. Comparison of Liquid Ratios, 1983–5

	Liquid ratios		Liquid ratios excluding short-term loans	
	British Vita group	Industry	British Vita group	Industry
1983	0·94	0·72	1·06	0·93
1984	0·79	0·70	1·06	0·84
1985	0·78	0·66	0·94	0·86

Source: British Vita figures from Table 7.4; Industry figures from MicroEXSTAT.

does the current ratio to some extent, on the method chosen to value the stock-in-trade.

MicroEXSTAT (see p. 59) excludes amounts owed by and owing to associated companies from, respectively, the numerator and denominator of the liquid ratio, and we shall follow this practice. In the Vita Group, cash at Zambian banks awaiting remittance approval is omitted from the 1984 figures. Table 7.4 explains the calculations. In this and other tables in this chapter, 1984 refers to the restated figures, which are not materially different from the original figures.

Tables 7.5 and 7.6 compare the British Vita group's current and liquid ratios with those of the plastic and rubber fabricators industry as a whole.

The general picture is one of steadily falling liquidity for both British Vita and the industry. The industry as a whole tends to

Table 7.7. Calculation of Defensive Intervals, British Vita group 1983–5

	Liquid assets (= col. (g) Table 7.4) (a) £000	Operating expenses requiring use of liquid assets (b) £000	Defensive interval (days) (c) = (a) ÷ (b) × 365
1983	27,262	106,497	93
1984	39,228	131,117	109
1985	50,334	181,536	101

have higher current ratios and lower liquid ratios than British Vita. A possible explanation of this is the latter's policy, already noted, of keeping finished goods stocks to a minimum.

Defensive or No Credit Interval

Both the current ratio and the liquid ratio are static rather than dynamic, that is, they treat liquidity as something to be measured at a point in time rather than over a period. A more dynamic approach would be to divide the liquid assets not by the current liabilities but by those operating expenses which require the use of liquid assets, namely, cost of sales, distribution costs, administrative expenses, interest and taxation (but not the dividends if the analysis is from the point of view of the shareholders). Depreciation if not included as it is not a cash expense. What is sought is a crude measure of how long a company could survive without borrowing if no receipts were coming in from debtors. The calculations for British Vita are shown in Table 7.7. The result of the calculation, measured in days by multiplying the ratio by 365, can be called the 'defensive (or no credit) interval'. It would be preferable to use forecast rather than past operating expenses, but these, of course, are not available to the external analyst.

Average Collection Period and Stock Turnover

Another important indicator of liquidity is the speed at which debts are collected. The average collection period for debtors

Table 7.8. Calculation of Average Collection Period and Stock Turnover, British Vita Group, 1983–5

	Sales (a) £000	Trade debtors (b) £000	Cost of sales (c) £000	Stocks (d) £000	Average collection period (b) ÷ (a) × 365 days	Stock turnover (c) ÷ (d)
1983	109,677	21,124	83,102	14,509	70	5·7
1984	133,950	33,029	104,137	19,530	90	5·3
1985	186,108	40,728	144,144	22,241	80	6·5

Source: British Vita PLC, Annual Report and Accounts, 1984 and 1985.

can be calculated as follows, if one assumes that all sales are for credit:

$$\frac{\text{trade debtors} \times 365}{\text{sales}} \text{ days}$$

Average debtors (defined as the mean of the opening and closing debtors figures) are also sometimes used. One problem with this ratio is that debtors include value added tax (VAT), whereas sales do not.

Another way of looking at the average collection period in terms of debtors turnover: $\frac{\text{sale}}{\text{debtors}}$. The relationship between stocks and cost of sales is usually looked at in this way: stock turnover $= \frac{\text{cost of sales}}{\text{stocks}}$. In assessing these ratios, it must be remembered that they are weighted averages. There are important differences per product and per geographical area which only more detailed accounts would reveal.

Table 7.8 shows how British Vita's average collection period and stock turnover can be calculated.

The average collection period relates to credit taken. A similar calculation for credit given can be made as follows:

$$\frac{\text{trade creditors} \times 365}{\text{cost of sales}} \text{ days}$$

Table 7.9. Calculation of Average Payment Period, British Vita Group, 1983–5

	Cost of sales (a)	Trade creditors (b)	Average payment period (b) ÷ (a) × 365 days
1983	83,102	17,748	78
1984	104,137	27,779	97
1985	144,144	35,857	91

Source: British Vita PLC, Annual Report and Accounts, 1984 and 1985.

Table 7.9 shows how the average payment period for British Vita is calculated.

It will be noted that British Vita's average collection periods are shorter than its average payment periods and have moved in much the same manner, as has also the stock turnover.

Predicting Insolvency

The extreme case of illiquidity is insolvency, which occurs when a company is unable to pay its debts as they fall due.

Can financial ratios be used to predict insolvency in advance? Researchers in both the USA and the UK have approached this problem by examining the ratios of companies just prior to their insolvency. It is possible by the use of statistical techniques to calculate what is known as a 'Z-score' for companies based on a number of relevant ratios appropriately weighted. Companies with scores within a certain range are more likely to become insolvent.

As is usual in ratio analysis, it is necessary to use more than one ratio and the result is a guide, not a certainty. A company with a bad score is not certain to become insolvent, but only more likely to.

Window-dressing

We end this chapter with an illustration of a problem which arises from the nature of ratios. Suppose that a company has current assets of £800,000, current liabilities of £500,000 and

Table 7.10. Illustration of Window-dressing

Current assets (a) £000	Current liabilities (b) £000	Liquid assets (c) £000	Current ratio (a) ÷ (b)	Liquid ratio (c) ÷ (b)
800	500	550	1·60	1·10
700	400	450	1·75	1·12
600	300	350	2·00	1·17
500	200	250	2·50	1·25
400	100	150	4·00	1·50
350	50	100	7·00	2·00
301	1	51	301·00	51·00

liquid assets of £550,000. Its *net* current assets and *net* liquid assets will therefore be £300,000 and £50,000 respectively. If we keep these *net* amounts constant but vary the gross figures using current assets to pay off current liabilities, then the current and liquid ratios will vary as shown in Table 7.10.

This is one example of window-dressing, which may be defined more generally as any transaction the purpose of which is to so arrange affairs that the financial statements of a company give a misleading or unrepresentative impression of its financial position. The example is exaggerated to make a point, but it is important to note that, within limits, companies may be able to arrange their current assets and liabilities so as to have the desired ratios at balance sheet time.

8. Sources of Funds and Capital Structure

Les affaires, c'est bien simple: c'est l'argent des autres
ALEXANDRE DUMAS, fils, *La Question d'argent*

Sources of Funds

The funds available to a company are obtained either from its shareholders or by borrowing. The former includes not only issues of shares but also the retention of profits. The latter range from long-term debt to trade credit. The composition at any time of these sources, and more especially the long-term sources, is referred to as the 'capital structure' of a company. Table 8.1 gives some idea of the relative importance of various sources for manufacturing companies in 1981 and 1982. Figures for British Vita (in rather more detail) for 1983, 1984 and 1985 are given in Table 8.2.

Four points in particular stand out from Table 8.1:

1. By far the most important source of funds is the ordinary shareholders, especially through the medium of reserves (which consist mainly of retained profits).
2. Preference shares are of very minor importance.
3. Deferred taxation is rather ambiguous: is it equity or debt or both? (See the discussion in Chapter 4.)
4. Long-term debt is important, although well behind reserves.

The importance of reserves is understated by the conventional use of historical costs, for, to the extent that tangible fixed assets and stocks are not shown at current costs, the revaluation reserve is smaller than it would otherwise be.

Table 8.1. Sources of Funds, UK Manufacturing Companies, 1981 and 1982

	1981		1982	
	£m	%	£m	%
Ordinary shares	12,755	15	13,330	15
Reserves	53,297	65	56,006	65
Ordinary shareholders' funds	66,052	80	69,336	80
Preference shares	782	1	827	1
Deferred taxation	2,546	3	2,596	3
Minority interests	4,058	5	4,853	6
Debentures, mortgages and long-term loans	8,707	11	8,952	10
	82,145	100	86,564	100
Bank loans and overdrafts	14,555		16,718	

Source: Calculated from *Company Finance*, Seventeenth Issue, 1986, Table 1.

Table 8.2. Sources of Funds, British Vita Group, 1983–5

	1983		1984*		1985	
	£000	%	£000	%	£000	%
Ordinary shares	6,819	13	7,532	12	7,550	12
Undistributable reserves	18,151	35	20,027	33	15,336	24
Distributable reserves	19,795	38	23,170	38	23,128	36
Ordinary shareholders' funds	44,765	86	50,729	83	46,014	73
Preference shares	57	0	57	0	57	0
Deferred liabilities and taxation	687	1	1,074	2	2,352	4
Minority interests	408	1	249	0	566	1
Debentures and bonds	1,235	2	1,071	2	945	1
Other long- and medium-term loans	4,953	10	8,313	14	13,436	21
Capital employed	52,105	100	61,493	100	63,370	100
Bank overdrafts	2,188		11,675		10,001	

* Restated.
Source: British Vita PLC, Annual Reports and Accounts, 1984 and 1985.

Table 8.2 shows the continuing importance of ordinary share-holders' funds to the British Vita group, but also an increase in long- and medium-term loans in 1985 accompanied by a decrease in undistributable reserves. More details of these movements are given in the Group Source and Application of Funds Statement [p. 14] and in the Notes [pp. 23 and 24]. The key items are the increase in medium-term loans mainly raised in foreign currencies and the negative exchange rate adjustments (which have been explained and discussed in Chapter 4).

Capital Structure

Is there such a thing as an optimal capital structure for a particular company? This is a question which has aroused much debate. In principle there probably is such a structure, but it is not simple in practice for a company either to discover what it is or to achieve it.

The main problem is to choose the best mix of debt (loans, debentures) and equity (ordinary shares, reserves, retained profits). There is no easy way of doing this. It is possible to list the factors which ought to be considered, but assessing the weight to be given to each remains very largely a matter of judgement and experience. The factors are:

1. *Cost:* The current and future cost of each potential source of capital should be estimated and compared. It should be borne in mind that costs of each source are not necessarily independent of each other. An increase in debt now, for example, may push up the cost of equity later. Other things being equal, it is desirable to minimize the average overall cost of capital to the company.
2. *Risk:* It is unwise (and often disastrous) to place a company in a position where it may be unable, if profits fall even temporarily, to pay interest as it falls due or to meet redemptions. It is equally undesirable to be forced to cut or omit the ordinary dividend (see the section below on dividend policy).
3. *Control:* Except where there is no alternative, a company should not make any issue of shares which will have the effect of removing or diluting control by the existing shareholders.

4. *Acceptability:* A company can only borrow if others are willing to lend to it. Few listed companies can afford the luxury of a capital structure which is unacceptable to financial institutions. A company with readily mortgageable assets will find it easier to raise debt.
5. *Transferability:* Shares may be listed or unlisted. Many private companies have made issues of shares to the public in order to obtain a stock exchange listing and to improve the transferability of their shares. Such a procedure may also have tax advantages.

Cost of capital and risk are discussed in more detail in the next two sections.

Cost of Capital

Although a company cannot always choose what appears to be the cheapest source of capital, because of the need to pay attention to risk, control, acceptability and transferability, it should always estimate the cost of each potential source and the effect on the overall average cost.

A rather over-simplified approach is to work out first of all the cost of each potential source of capital. This is most easily done in the case of debentures. Suppose that a company can issue £100,000 10 per cent debentures at par, repayable at par in twenty years' time. The before-tax cost is obviously 10 per cent; the after-tax cost, assuming immediate payment and a corporation tax rate of 35 per cent, is 6·5 per cent. If preference shares are issued instead, the before- and after-tax rates would be equal, since preference dividends, unlike debenture interest, are not deductible for tax purposes. This explains why, since the introduction of corporation tax in 1965, many companies have replaced their preference share capital by loan stock. The introduction of the imputation system, however, has made preference shares a little more attractive.

The arithmetic becomes rather more difficult if the loan stock is not issued at par. In December 1970, for example, Imperial Chemical Industries P L C made an issue of £40 million 10·75 per cent unsecured loan stock 1991/6 at £98 per cent, payable £20 per £100 stock on application, £40 on 1 March 1971 and £38 on 29 April 1971. That is, for every £98 received over the period December 1970 to April 1971 the company promised to pay interest of £10·75 each year and to repay the stock at par (£100) between 1991 and 1996. Using tables (or a computer program), it can be calculated that the yield to the last redemption date (1996) was a fraction under 11 per cent.

The real cost of issuing debentures is reduced during a period of inflation by the fact that the cash paid out by the company will be of lower purchasing power than the cash it receives at the date of issue.

Reckoning the cost of an issue of ordinary shares is more difficult. An analogous calculation to the one above would suggest that it is equal to the gross dividend yield, worked out as follows:

$$\frac{\text{current dividend per ordinary share} \times 100}{\text{market price per share}} \times \frac{100}{71}$$

The purpose of multiplying by 100/71 is to allow for the tax credit.

Dividend yields may be most easily found from the stock exchange pages of the *Financial Times* and other newspapers. The *Financial Times* Share Information Service gives quite a lot of information about shares every day. The following typical entry has been extracted from the *Financial Times* of 12 April 1986 (referring to the day before):

1986					Div.		Yield	
high	low	Stock	Price	+ or −	net	Cover	gross	P/E
322	195	British Vita	315		7·0	3·1	3·1	13·4

This tells us that the current market price of British Vita's ordinary shares (par value 25p) is 315p, compared with a high for the year of 322p, a low of 195p and a price the day before of 315p. (Par values may be assumed to be 25p unless the *Financial Times* states otherwise.) The most recent dividend was 7·0p per share.

British Vita's dividend yield (gross) is calculated by the *Financial Times* as follows:

$$\frac{\text{current dividend per ordinary share} \times 100}{\text{market price per share}} \times \frac{100}{71}$$

That is to say:

$$\frac{7 \cdot 0 \times 100}{315} \times \frac{100}{71} = 3 \cdot 1\%.$$

The dividend yield of any company can be compared with dividend yields in general and with those of other companies in the same equity group or sub-section, by looking at the table in the *Financial Times* headed 'FT – Actuaries Share Indices'. On 11 August 1986 the '500 Share' dividend yield was 4·04 per cent.

These yields can be contrasted with the 9·23 per cent yield on irredeemable government stocks and a redemption yield of 10·57 per cent on 25-year redeemable debentures and loans. Given the relative riskiness of fixed-interest and variable-dividend securities, this is at first sight surprising. Before August 1959, in fact, the average dividend yield was higher than the yield on government bonds. Since then a 'reverse yield gap', as it is called, has existed. The main reason for the reverse yield gap is the realization by investors that equities offer more protection against the effects of inflation. This has raised share prices relatively and lowered yields.

The dividend yield cannot, however, be regarded as an adequate measure of the cost of equity capital. It fails to take account of the facts that future dividends may be different from the current dividend and that the price of the shares may change. Neither of these considerations is relevant to long-term debt with its fixed interest payments and fixed redemption prices.

Two possible measures of the cost of equity capital are the *earnings yield* and the *dividend yield plus a growth rate*. The earnings yield is calculated as follows:

$$\frac{\text{earnings per ordinary share after tax} \times 100}{\text{market price per ordinary share}}$$

It is usual to express the same relationship in the form of a *price–earnings ratio* (P/E ratio), which is simply the reciprocal of the earnings yield multiplied by 100, that is:

$$\frac{\text{market price per ordinary share}}{\text{earnings per ordinary share after tax}}$$

In other words, the P/E ratio expresses the multiple of the last reported earnings that the market is willing to pay for the ordinary shares. The higher the P/E ratio (the lower the earnings yield), the more the market thinks of the company and the cheaper the cost of equity capital to the company.

From the extract from the *Financial Times* it can be seen that British Vita's price-earnings ratio on 11 August 1986 was 13·4. The 500 share figure was 13·18.

It is necessary to look a little more closely here at some of the problems of calculating earnings per share (EPS) and hence the P/E ratio. Earnings are calculated *before* the deduction of extraordinary items (discussed on p. 27) but after the deduction of tax and preference dividends. The tax charge, however, depends to some extent on the dividends declared, since there are both constant and variable components in the tax charge.

The statement of standard accounting practice on earnings per share (SSAP 3), which unlike most SSAPs applies only to listed companies, distinguishes between the 'net basis' and the 'nil basis'. The former takes account of both constant and variable components and has the obvious advantage that all the relevant facts are considered. The latter takes account only of the constant components (that is, it in effect assumes a nil distribution of dividends). Its advantage is that it produces an EPS which is independent of the level of dividend distribution. For most companies the two bases will in practice give the same result. This is not likely to be the case, however, for companies relying heavily on overseas income. SSAP 3 concludes that companies should use the net basis in their annual reports but should also show the figure arrived at on a nil basis where the difference is material. The *Financial Times* calculates P/E ratios on a net basis, putting the resulting figure in brackets if calculation on a nil basis results in a difference of 10 per cent or more. (European Ferries P L C is an example of this in the *Financial Times* of 12 August 1986.) The *Financial Times* calculations also assume an A C T rate equal to the basic rate of income tax.

The British Vita earnings per share figures are calculated on a net basis. The 1985 calculation is as follows:

$$\text{EPS} = \frac{\text{profit before extraordinary items}}{\text{weighted average of ordinary shares}}$$
$$= \frac{£7,084,000}{£30,138,283} = 23 \cdot 5\text{p.}$$

The P/E ratio is therefore:

$$\frac{\text{market price per share}}{\text{EPS}} = \frac{315}{23 \cdot 5} = 13 \cdot 4.$$

Companies also publish a 'fully diluted' EPS figure where this is materially different from the 'basic' EPS. Dilution can arise from the existence of shares that may rank for dividend in the future, from convertible loan stock (see p. 97) and from options and warrants.

The final figure which needs to be explained is British Vita's dividend cover, which according to the *Financial Times* is 3·1. Since the market is interested in future dividends, it prefers to see current dividends reasonably well covered by current earnings. This is some sort of guarantee that the dividends will be at least maintained in future since, if profits fall, there will be past retained profits to draw upon. The *Financial Times* measure of dividend cover is:

EPS on a maximum basis
ordinary dividend per share

EPS on a maximum basis is yet a third approach to this somewhat elusive concept. It is based on the assumption (seldom, of course, the reality) that a company distributes *all* its profits and is liable to pay ACT on them. This produces a dividend cover of 3·1 as distinct from the 1·8 (= 3,715/2,114) given on page 10 of British Vita's 1985 report.

An alternative approach to the cost of equity capital is to add a growth rate to the dividend yield. If one considers, for example, that British Vita's dividends are likely to grow in future at an average annual rate of 8 per cent, then the cost of its equity capital would be estimated to be 3·1 per cent plus 8 per cent, which equals 11·1 per cent.

An approach to the cost of a company's equity capital strongly favoured in the literature on financial theory is that it is equal to:

$$R_f + \beta[E(R_m) - R_f].$$

where R_f is the return on a riskless security (for example, a treasury bill), $E(R_m)$ is the expected return on all the securities in the market and β (beta) is a measure of risk.

The meaning and measurement of beta is discussed in the next section.

Risk: Betas and Gearing

Risk is of two kinds: market (or systematic) risk and specific (or non-market) risk. Market risk can be quantified as the beta of a company's ordinary shares. Beta measures the sensitivity of the share price to movements in the market. British Vita's beta at the end of 1985 was estimated by the London Business School Risk Measurement Service to be 1·14. A beta of 1·14 means that the share will on average move 1·14 per cent for each 1 per cent move by the market. A share with a beta of 1·0 would on average move in line with the market. In 1985 betas ranged from

1·40 to 0·25. The beta of Saga Holidays, for example, was 1·01. Industry betas are also available: 0·86 for plastic and rubber fabricators and 0·87 for leisure companies in 1985 if the component companies are equally weighted.

Specific risk refers to factors specific to a company and is measured as a percentage return per annum. The higher the percentage, the greater the specific risk. Property companies tend to have a high specific risk and investment trusts a low one. In 1985 specific risk figures ranged from 104 per cent down to 8 per cent, with an average of about 25 per cent. British Vita's and Saga Holidays' figures were 19 per cent and 37 per cent respectively. The industry figures were 40 per cent and 39 per cent on an equally weighted basis.

The distinction between market risk and specific risk is important because it is possible to reduce the latter by diversification (for example, by holding shares in both plastics and rubber fabricators and in leisure companies), but market risk cannot be diversified away. Both British Vita and Saga Holidays are affected by the general state of the economy.

Betas can be measured from either market data ('market betas') or from accounting data ('accounting betas'). The London Business School at present calculates only the former, comparing the monthly returns (dividend yield plus capital appreciation) for the last five years on each share with the corresponding returns on the market index. Betas do, of course, change over time, although most are reasonably stationary.

The more traditional accounting measure of risk is gearing. Companies with the highest betas tend to be highly geared and to come from highly cyclical industries.

Gearing (or 'leverage', as the Americans call it) is the relationship between the funds provided to a company by its ordinary shareholders and the long-term sources of funds carrying a fixed interest charge or dividend (for example, unsecured loans, debentures and preference shares). The degree of gearing can be measured in terms of either capital or income. A company's capital structure is said to be highly geared when the fixed charges claim an above-average proportion of the company's resources of either capital or income.

There is more than one way of defining and calculating a 'gearing ratio'. If we define it as:

$$\frac{\text{interest-bearing liabilities} + \text{preference shares}}{\text{ordinary shareholders' funds}} \times 100\%$$

we can calculate the following ratios from Tables 8.1 and 8.2:

	Manufacturing companies %	British Vita group %
1981	14	n/a
1982	14	n/a
1983	n/a	14
1984	n/a	19
1985	n/a	31

Alternatively, we could add back overdrafts and loans to the numerator on the grounds that, to a large extent, they may be renewed each year and therefore should be treated as long-term sources of funds, even though included under the heading of current liabilities in *Company Finance*.

The relevant figures are also given in Tables 8.1 and 8.2. The gearing ratios now become:

	Manufacturing companies %	British Vita group %
1981	36	n/a
1982	38	n/a
1983	n/a	19
1984	n/a	42
1985	n/a	53

Under either definition British Vita has clearly become more highly geared. Note 18 [p. 23] shows that between 1984 and 1985 this has occurred mainly through an increase in medium-term loans.

Both the above definitions are based on book values. Market values could (some would say 'should') be used instead if they are available. The definition would now become:

$$\frac{\text{market value of fixed interest securities}}{\text{market value of ordinary share capital}}$$

Whichever way the calculation is made, some companies are more highly geared than others, especially those which have relatively stable profits, and assets, such as land and buildings, which can be specifically identified and are unlikely to fall in value over time, therefore providing good security.

'Times interest earned' is really just a different way of looking at gearing. It is defined as:

$$\frac{\text{profit on ordinary activities before interest and tax}}{\text{interest (gross)}}$$

sing the data on page 10 of the 1985 report and adjusting for interest received, times interest earned can be calculated for British Vita as follows:

$$1983 \quad \frac{11,647}{1,071} = 10 \cdot 9 \text{ times}$$

$$1984 \quad \frac{11,885}{1,437} = 8 \cdot 3 \text{ times}$$

$$1985 \quad \frac{14,640}{2,409} = 6 \cdot 1 \text{ times}$$

All the measures show British Vita becoming more highly geared.

The major disadvantage of the 'times interest earned' method is that it ignores the existence of reserves, that is, the retained profits of previous years, upon which the company could call if necessary (if they are in liquid form). The same drawback applies to the 'priority percentages' approach, in which the analyst calculates the percentage of earnings that is required to service each category of loan and share capital.

The effect of gearing on profits available to ordinary shareholders can be seen from the following example.

X PLC is a very highly geared company and Y PLC a

relatively low geared one. Their long term sources of funds are
as follows:

	X	Y
Ordinary share capital (par value)	100,000	200,000
Retained profit	100,000	200,000
Ordinary shareholders' funds	200,000	400,000
10% debenture	300,000	100,000
	£500,000	£500,000
Gearing ratio (debentures as % of ordinary shareholders' funds)	150%	25%

If profit before interest and tax is £80,000 for both companies,
the distributable profit will be as follows, assuming a 35 per
cent tax rate:

	X	Y
(a) Profit before interest and tax	80,000	80,000
(b) Debenture interest (gross)	30,000	10,000
	50,000	70,000
Tax at 35%	17,500	24,500
Distributable profit	32,500	45,500
Times interest earned (a ÷ b)	2·67	8·00

Distributable profit will be 32·5 per cent of the par value for
Company X and 22·75 per cent for Company Y.

If, however, the profit before interest and tax is £160,000, the
position will be as follows:

	X	Y
(a) Profit before interest and tax	160,000	160,000
(b) Debenture interest (gross)	30,000	10,000
	130,000	150,000
Tax at 35%	45,500	52,500

Distributable profit	84,500	97,500
Times interest earned (a ÷ b)	5·33	16·00

Distributable profit as a proportion of the par value becomes 84·5 per cent for Company X and 48·75 per cent for Company Y. Note that while profits before interest and tax have doubled, X's distributable profit as a percentage of par value has gone up 2·60 times and Y's 2·14 times. It is clear that gearing enables a company to trade on the equity, as the Americans say, and to increase the ordinary shareholders' return at a faster rate than the increase in profits. The higher the gearing, the greater the relative rate.

Unfortunately, the converse also applies. Suppose that the profit before interest and tax falls to £30,000. The position will then be as follows:

	X	Y
(a) Profit before interest and tax	30,000	30,000
(b) Debenture interest (gross)	30,000	10,000
	—	20,000
Tax at 35%	—	7,000
Distributable profit	£—	£13,000
Times interest earned (a ÷ b)	1·00	3·00

The distributable profit as a proportion of par value of Company X falls to zero and of Company Y to 6·5 per cent. If profits fell even further, Company X would not be able to pay the debenture interest out of its current profits and would have to call upon past retained profits (reserves). Once these were exhausted, it would be in serious trouble. Company Y is in a much better position to meet such an emergency. It must also be remembered, of course, that a company which has tied up its assets too much in fixed assets and stocks may run into similar problems even though its profits have not fallen. Profits are not the same thing as ready cash.

The moral is that companies whose profits are low or likely to fluctuate violently should not be too highly geared. Investors in such companies are running risks and will in any case prefer ordinary shares to fixed-interest debentures. From a company point of view the attraction of a relatively cheap source of funds must be balanced against the risks involved.

Dividend Policy

How does a company determine the size of the dividend it pays each year, or, putting the same question round the other way, how does a company decide how much of its profits to retain each year?

Retained profits are the most convenient source of funds, and a company which pays very high dividends loses this source and may have to raise money in the capital market. Issues of debentures and other loans usually have a lower cost of capital than either new issues of shares or retained profits, but, as we have just seen, there are dangers in a too highly geared capital structure. New issues of shares are more expensive than retained profits because of the issue costs involved.*

On the other hand, most expanding companies will have to go to the market sooner or later, and one of the points that potential investors will look at is the dividend record. A company whose dividend has declined or fluctuated violently is not likely to be favourably regarded. For this reason companies prefer to maintain their dividends even if earnings fall. Dividends have an information content; that is, they alter or confirm investors' beliefs about the future prospects of a company.

On the whole, then, cost of capital considerations push companies towards constant or steadily increasing dividend payouts. Inflation may have the same effect if the directors of a company feel that the distribution to shareholders ought to keep pace with the decline in the purchasing power of money. It may also have the opposite effect if the directors feel the need to retain a

* Retained profits are not a costless source of funds. They can be regarded as a notional distribution of profits which are immediately re-invested in the company.

Table 8.3. British Vita PLC; Earnings and Dividend Record, 1981–5

	1981	1982	1983	1984	1984 restated	1985
Profit attributable to ordinary shareholders (£000)	3,809	3,269	6,157	6,361	5,684	3,715
Index (1981 = 100)	100	86	162	167	149	98
Earnings per ordinary share:*	15.0p	12.7p	22.0p	24.3p	22.0p	23.5p
Ordinary dividend (£000)	1,444	1,464	1,609	1,868	1,868	2,114
Index (1981 = 100)	100	101	111	129	129	146
Dividend per ordinary share*	4.91p	4.91p	5.36p	6.2p	6.2p	7.00p
Dividend cover	2.6	2.2	3.8	3.4	3.0	1.8
Index of retail prices (average for calendar year)	295	320	335	352	352	373

* Adjusted for the capitalization issue.
Sources: British Vita PLC, Annual Report and Accounts; *Accountancy*, December 1986.

higher proportion of historical cost earnings in order to maintain operating capacity. Two factors which tend to limit the size of the dividend are government policy and taxation. A number of governments since the war, in their efforts to contain rises in wages and prices, have placed statutory limitations on the size of company dividends. In spite of capital gains tax, the British tax system still favours capital increases rather than income increases. There are many shareholders who are more interested in capital gains than dividends. In general, shareholders are likely to be attracted to companies which have a dividend policy suited to their needs. This is known as the 'clientele effect'.

We are now in a position to look at British Vita's dividend policy. Table 8.3 gives information about the group's dividend policy for the last five years. It has been adapted from the information given on page 10 of the 1985 Report. All the information is on a historical cost basis. It is interesting to compare the earnings record with the dividend record. When earnings per share (EPS) fell in 1982, dividend per share (DPS) was held constant. When EPS increased considerably in 1983, DPS increased also, but by no means to the same extent. The fall in EPS in 1985 was matched by a rise in DPS which the chairman justified by expectations of future growth [p. 5]. The 1986 interim report (Appendix D) announced EPS for the first half of 1986 up 34 per cent on the first half of 1985 and an interim dividend up 21 per cent on 1985. A comparison of DPS and the retail price index shows that for the period 1981 to 1985 the former increased by 46 per cent, the latter by 26 per cent; that is, dividends per share fell in real terms.

Rights Issues and Capitalization Issues

Most issues of shares are either rights issues or capitalization issues. A rights issue is one in which existing shareholders are given a chance to subscribe before anybody else. If they do not wish to do so, they can sell their rights on the market. Rights issues have long been the norm, and since 1980 it has been obligatory for share issues by public companies to be rights issues unless the shareholders pass a resolution to the contrary.

British Vita has made both rights and capitalization issues in recent years. The company made a rights issue in 1980: 5,286,849 new ordinary shares of 25p each were offered on the basis of one new ordinary share for every four ordinary shares held on 1 September 1980. The offer price, fixed as usual a little below the current market price, was 105p per share. 27·5 per cent of the issue was placed with a number of institutions at a price of 16p per share (nil paid) on behalf of certain directors and substantial shareholders who did not wish to take up all their rights.

The effect of the rights issue on British Vita's balance sheet (ignoring the issue costs of approximately £190,000) was as follows:

	£000
Increase in cash balances (5,286,849 × 105p)	5,551
Represented by	
increase in share capital (at par) (5,286,849 × 25p	1,322
increase in share premium (5,286,849 × 80p)	4,229
	5,551

The purpose of the issue was announced by the board of directors to be to enlarge the capital base so that the group retained the flexibility to respond quickly to opportunities as they arose while maintaining an appropriate balance between equity and debt.

When dealings commenced for the nil-paid shares, the price fluctuated between 10p and 18p. A nil-paid price of 16p assumed a market price of 125p before the issue. The value of all the existing shares at this price was $4 \times 5,286,849 \times £1.25 = £26,434,245$. Adding the cash receipts from the new shares $(5,286,849 \times £1.05 = £5,551,191)$ gave a new total of $£31,985,436$. Dividing this by the new number of shares $(5 \times 5,286,849 = 26,434,245)$ resulted in a new value per share of 121p (105p + 16p).

An existing shareholder who sold his rights for 16p was no worse off than one who took up his rights at 105p. Assume a shareholder (male) with 4,000 shares and £1,050 in cash. If he used the cash to take up his rights, he would have 5,000 shares valued at 121p (£6,050). If he sold his rights for 16p per new share, he would have 4,000 shares valued £4,840 and £1,210 in cash (the original £1,050 plus £160 from the sale), that is, £6,050. A shareholder who took no action had his rights automatically sold in the market and received the proceeds net of expenses of sale.

A capitalization issue (also known as a 'scrip issue', a 'bonus issue' and, in the USA, a 'stock dividend') is simply a means of turning reserves into share capital. To clear up the misunderstandings which can arise from this, it is helpful to use a simple example. Consider a company whose summarized balance sheet is as follows:

Assets	150,000	Ordinary share capital	
		(40,000 shares of £1 each)	40,000
less Liabilities	50,000	Reserves	60,000
	£100,000		£100,000

The company decides to make a capitalization issue of one

new share for two old shares. The balance sheet will now look like this:

Assets	150,000	Ordinary share capital	
		(60,000 shares of £1 each)	60,000
less Liabilities	50,000	Reserves	40,000
	£100,000		£100,000

All that has happened is a book entry. In order to increase the ordinary share capital from £40,000 to £60,000, the accountant has decreased the reserves from £60,000 to £40,000. The shareholders have not received any cash, only more paper. Are they any better off? In principle, no; the market price *per share* might beexpected to fall proportionately. It may not do so, partly because unrelated factors may be affecting share prices at the same time, partly because the issue may have drawn favourable attention to the future prospects of the company. Of course, if the company announces at the same time that the total amount to be paid out in dividends to shareholders will be increased, then the shareholders really are better off and the market price will tend to rise.

Capitalization issues have to be adjusted for when making comparisons of earnings per share (EPS). In this example, if the earnings were £12,000 the EPS before the capitalization issue is 30p; after the issue it is 20p.

British Vita used part of its share premium in 1984 to make a capitalization issue. 2,728,029 ordinary shares of 25p were allotted to existing shareholders fully paid, decreasing the share premium account (an undistributable reserve) by approximately £682,000 and increasing share capital by the same amount.

The 1986 Interim Report (Appendix D) announces a 1 for 2 capitalization issue.

Convertible Loan Stock

So far in this book we have drawn a rather rigid dividing line between debenture-holders, who are merely long-term creditors of a company, and shareholders, who are its owners. It will have been apparent, however, that preference share capital has some of the characteristics of long-term debt. Another hybrid security of importance is the convertible loan.

The 1986 annual report of Whitbread and Co. PLC, for example, includes the following item among the long-term loan capital:

11½% convertible unsecured loan stock 1990/95 – £12·97 million

---

The attraction of such stock to an investor is that it enables him to buy a fixed-interest stock which he can later change into ordinary shares if he so wishes. Whether he will make the conversion or not depends, of course, on the relationship between the market price of the ordinary shares and the conversion price at the conversion date. The investor's hope is that he has found a cheaper way of buying the ordinary shares than direct purchase. The disadvantage to him is that the rate of interest offered on a convertible loan is less than that on a 'straight' loan.

Why should a company issue convertible stock? There are at least two possibilities:

---

1. The company wants to issue debt and adds the convertibility as an added attraction.
2. The company would prefer to issue equity but feels that the price of its ordinary shares is temporarily depressed. By setting the conversion price higher than the current price, the management can, if its expectations are fulfilled, effectively make a share issue at the desired price.

The possible disadvantages to the company are that either the market price fails to rise and it is saddled with unwanted debt, or that the market price rises so quickly that it finds itself in effect selling equity more cheaply than it need have done. As already noted, the existence of convertible loan stock dilutes the basic earnings per share.

Leasing

Instead of borrowing money to buy fixed assets, a company may decide to lease them; that is, to enter into a long-term contract which allows it the use of the asset (but does not give it the ownership) in return for a periodic rental. Early termination of the lease is penalized. Sometimes the company already owns the assets and raises cash by selling them and then leasing them back. This is known as sale-and-leaseback.

The effect in either case is similar to an issue of long-term debt and it should be regarded and analysed as such. It is now standard accounting practice for finance leases (leases that transfer substantially all the risks and rewards of ownership to the lessee) to be capitalized. This means that both the leased asset and the long-term liability to pay the lease rentals are shown in the balance sheet. Operating leases are not capitalized. The amount of operating lease rentals paid each year has to be disclosed in the Notes. British Vita discloses a figure of £719,000 in 1985 [p. 17].

As in all financing decisions, the effect on the tax payable by the company is an important factor in deciding whether or not to use leasing. If equipment is bought out of borrowed money, the company will be entitled to the capital allowances described in Chapter 3, and the interest on the loan will be tax-deductible. If the equipment is leased, the lessor will receive the benefit of the capital allowances, but the lessee's annual taxable income will be reduced by the amount of the lease rental. It is not possible to state in general terms whether the tax effect will be favourable or unfavourable to the prospective lessee. Each case has to be analysed separately.

9. Summary and Reading Guide

The reader who has come this far has already learned a great deal about the annual reports of companies, about financial statements and about accounting and finance. The purpose of this chapter is to summarize what has been learned and to make suggestions about further reading.

Companies

Chapter 1 was mainly about companies, the most important form of business organization in modern Britain. Over 99 per cent of all companies are private, but public companies are of greater economic significance. It is with public companies, and especially with those that are listed on the stock exchange, that investors are mainly concerned. Published annual reports are typically those of groups of companies, consisting of a holding company, subsidiaries, sub-subsidiaries and associated companies.

Companies operate within the legal framework of the Companies Act 1985 and relevant case law. There are many good text books on company law. An introductory one which can be recommended is Smith and Keenan, *Company Law* (Pitman, 6th edn, 1986). More advanced is R. R. Pennington, *Company Law* (Butterworths, 5th edn, 1985).

Financial Statements

Chapter 2 dealt with financial statements. The three most important statements are:

---

1. *The balance sheet*, which shows the assets, the liabilities and the shareholders' funds at a particular date.
2. *The profit and loss account* (or income statement), which shows for an accounting period the revenues, expenses, net profit (before and after taxation) and often also the distribution of the profit.
3. *The sources and application of funds statement* (funds statement), which shows the sources and uses of funds of a company over the same accounting period.

Assets are classified into *fixed* and *current*, and liabilities classified according to whether they fall due within one year or more than one year. The excess of current assets over current liabilities is the working capital of a company. Tangible fixed assets are depreciated over their estimated economic lives, depreciation in its accounting sense normally referring to the allocation over time of the cost less estimated scrap value.

Long-term sources of funds of companies can be divided into *loan capital* (for example, debentures) on the one hand, and *shareholders' funds* (share capital and reserves) on the other. There is an important distinction between preference shares, usually carrying a fixed dividend rate and having priority in a winding up, and ordinary shares, which form the *equity* of the company. The par or face value of a share is not necessarily the same as its issue price (issues are often made at a premium) or its market price.

The profit and loss account is drawn up from the point of view of the shareholders. Much the same information can be used to prepare a statement of value added, which shows how wealth has been created by the operations of the group and how that wealth has been allocated.

The source and application of funds statement demonstrates among other things the difference between increases in profit and increases in cash balances. Cash flow is a rather imprecise term, often meaning simply net profit plus depreciation and other items not involving the movement of funds.

A good introductory book on accounting and financial statements is C. Nobes, *Introduction to Financial Accounting* (Allen & Unwin, rev. edn, 1983). There are a number of more advanced books, such as R. Lewis and D. Pendrill, *Advanced Financial Accounting* (Pitman, 2nd edn, 1985), and T. A. Lee (ed.), *Developments in Accounting* (Philip Allan, 1981). Many of the large accounting firms publish excellent guides (continually revised) to the requirements of company law and accounting standards. Examples are Touche Ross & Co.'s *Reporting & Accounting Manual* (1985) and *Accounting Provisions of the Companies Act 1985* (Farringdon Publishing, 1985) by B. Johnson and M. Patient of Deloitte Haskins & Sells.

Taxation

Chapter 3 dealt briefly with taxation and audit. Companies pay corporation tax, not income tax. Taxable income is measured in much the same way as accounting profit, with the major exception of capital allowances (which replace depreciation). The corporation tax rate refers to a financial year which ends on 31 March, but companies are assessed on the basis of their own accounting periods.

Under the UK's imputation system, companies pay advance corporation tax when a dividend is paid and the shareholder receives a tax credit.

In general, taxable income has tended to be less than accounting profit. The total amount of taxation so 'deferred' is disclosed in the Notes but only included in the balance sheet to the extent that it is regarded as a liability.

Books on taxation tend to be written either for accountants (lots of figures), for lawyers (lots of case law) or for economists (lots of diagrams). Two books rather more readable and stimulating than most are J. A. Kay and M. A. King, *The British Tax System* (Oxford University Press, 4th edn, 1986), and S. James and C. Nobes, *The Economics of Taxation* (Philip Allan, 3rd edn, 1988).

Audit

The main function of the auditors of a company is to report to the shareholders whether in their opinion the financial statements show a true and fair view. A good introductory book is M. Sherer and D. Kent, *Auditing and Accountability* (Pitman, 1983).

Regulation, Formats, Accounting Standards and Inflation

Regulation, formats, accounting standards and inflation accounting were discussed in Chapter 4.

In Britain, decisions about disclosure, presentation and valuation are mainly in the hands of the government, through company law, and the accountancy profession, through statements of standard accounting practice issued by the Accounting Standards Committee.

Financial statements are based mainly on historical costs modified by prudence, but inflation accounting has been extensively debated (and even practised) in recent years.

As noted in Chapter 5, all extant accounting standards and exposure drafts are reproduced in *Accounting Standards*, revised annually and published by the Institute of Chartered Accountants in England and Wales. The best short book on inflation accounting is G. Whittington, *Inflation Accounting: An Introduction to the Debate* (Cambridge University Press, 1983). A number of classic articles are brought together in R. H. Parker, G. C. Harcourt and G. Whittington (eds.), *Readings in the Concept and Measurement of Income* (Philip Allan, 2nd edn, 1986).

Tools of Analysis

Chapter 5 was concerned with defining and explaining the uses and limitations of ratios, percentages and yields as tools for the analysis of financial statements. George Foster, *Financial State-*

ment Analysis (Prentice-Hall, 2nd edn, 1986) is a very thorough treatment of the subject. There are relevant chapters in the books by Nobes and by Lewis and Pendrill already referred to, and in John Sizer, *An Insight into Management Accounting* (Penguin, 2nd edn, 1979).

Profitability, Return on Investment and Value Added

Profitability, return on investment and value added were discussed in Chapter 6, in which the relationships between sales, profits and assets were considered.

Liquidity and Cash Flows

In Chapter 7 it was pointed out that a company must be liquid as well as profitable and that making profits is not the same as accumulating cash. It was shown that the best way to control liquidity from inside the company is by means of a cash budget. The external analyst uses the current ratio and the liquid ratio as rather cruder measures. Other indicators of liquidity are the defensive interval, the average collection period and stock turnover. The extreme case of illiquidity is insolvency; some success has been achieved in predicting this by means of financial ratios.

Sources of Funds and Capital Structure

Chapter 8 discussed sources of funds and capital structure. It was pointed out that shareholders are still the most important source of long-term funds, especially through the medium of retained profits, but that loan capital is also of importance.

The problem of capital structure is to obtain the best mix of debt and equity. Factors to be considered are cost, risk, control, acceptability and transferability. It was argued that either the earnings yield (reciprocal of the price-earnings ratio) or the dividend yield plus a growth rate are better measures of the cost of equity than the dividend yield itself. The imputation system of corporate taxation has greatly complicated the calculation of measures of earnings per share.

Risk can be approached through traditional measures of gearing or through the calculation of betas, which quantify the market risk of a share as distinguished from its specific risk.

In deciding on its dividend policy, a company looks at its effects on the cost of capital, on dividend yield and on dividend cover and has to take account of government policy, inflation and taxation. Most companies try to pay a constant or moderately increased dividend (in money terms) each year, ironing out fluctuations in earnings.

Rights issues give existing shareholders the first chance to subscribe to new issues. They are distinguished from bonus issues, where the existing shareholders receive extra shares without further subscription.

The chapter ended with brief references to two other sources of funds: convertible loan stock and leasing.

There are a number of good books on the topics discussed in Chapters 6, 7 and 8, notably J. M. Samuels and F. M. Wilkes, *Management of Company Finance* (Van Nostrand Reinhold, 4th edn, 1986), and R. A. Brealey and S. Myers, *Principles of Corporate Finance* (McGraw-Hill, 2nd edn, 1984).

Personal Investment

This book has not dealt, except incidentally, with problems of personal investment. Its primary purpose has been to explain and interpret company annual reports and financial statements, not to advise the reader directly on how to invest his or her money on the stock market. It is not perhaps out of place, however, to conclude by recommending a book which does do this: N. Tait (ed.), *The Investors Chronicle Beginner's Guide to the Stock Market* (Penguin, 2nd edn, 1987).

Appendix A. Debits and Credits (Double Entry)

Most people know that accountants are concerned with debits and credits. Since it is possible to learn quite a lot about accounting and finance without using these terms, it has not been thought necessary to explain their meaning within the body of this book. Very little extra effort is required, however, to master double entry, so a brief explanation is given in this appendix.

It will be remembered that the following symbols were used in Chapter 2:

a	= assets	r	= revenues (e.g. sales, fees)
l	= liabilities	e	= expenses other than taxation
c	= shareholders' funds	t	= taxation
s	= share capital	d	= dividends
p	= retained profits	Δ	= net increase in

The identity for any balance sheet is

$$a = l + c$$

which can be expanded to

$$a = l + s + p$$

An increase on the left-hand side of the identity is called a debit (abbreviated to Dr.), an increase on the right-hand side a credit (abbreviated to Cr.). Similarly, decreases on the left-hand side are credits, and decreases on the right-hand side are debits. Debit and credit are used here as technical terms and should not be confused with any other meanings of these words.

In Chapter 2 we showed that an increase in retained profits (Δp) is equal to revenue less expenses, tax and dividends:

$$\Delta p = r - e - t - d$$

Now, since increases in retained profits are credits, it follows that increases in revenues are also credits, whereas increases in expenses, taxes and dividends must be debits. Conversely, decreases in revenues are debits and decreases in expenses, taxes and dividends are credits.

We can sum up the rules as follows:

DEBITS ARE:		CREDITS ARE:	
Increases in:	assets	*Increases in:*	liabilities
	expenses		share capital
	taxes		retained profits
	dividends		revenues
Decreases in:	liabilities	*Decreases in:*	assets
	share capital		expenses
	retained profits		taxes
	revenues		dividends

It seems curious at first sight that both increases in assets and expenses are debits. In fact, assets and expenses are much more closely linked than is usually realized. If a company buys for cash a machine which is expected to last ten years, it is rightly regarded as having acquired the asset machine (increase in machines, therefore debit 'machines') in exchange for the asset cash (decrease in cash, therefore credit 'cash'). Suppose, however, that technological change is so rapid that these machines have an economic life of only one year or less. Then, if the accounting period is one year, the machine can be regarded as an expense of the period (therefore, debit 'machine expense', credit 'cash').

Thus, in one sense, an asset is merely an expense paid for in advance which needs to be spread over several accounting periods in the form of depreciation.

The system of debits and credits is referred to as double entry, since maintenance of the accounting identity ($a = l + c$ in its simplest form) requires that any increase or decrease in one item be balanced by a corresponding increase or decrease in another item or items. There are always two sides to any transaction. Suppose, for example, that a company decreases its cash by £100. The other side of the transaction might be:

---

1. An increase in another asset such as a machine (so, debit 'machine', credit 'cash').
2. A decrease in a liability, such as a trade creditor (so, debit 'creditor', credit 'cash').
3. An increase in a negative capital item such as expenses, taxes or dividends (so, debit 'expenses', 'taxes' or 'dividends', credit 'cash').

Note that cash is always credited (since the asset cash has been decreased) and that a negative credit is the same as a debit (and a negative debit the same as a credit).

Appendix B. Glossary of Accounting and Financial Terms

This glossary serves two purposes:

1. To collect in alphabetical order various definitions, descriptions and explanations scattered throughout the text.
2. To provide certain *additional* information, especially concerning those matters which must by law be disclosed in the published financial statements of companies.

For more detail see R. H. Parker, *Macmillan Dictionary of Accounting* (Macmillan Press, 1984).

ACCELERATED DEPRECIATION: The writing off of depreciation (e.g., for tax purposes) at a faster rate than is justified by the rate of use of the asset concerned.

ACCOUNTING CONCEPTS: The assumptions which underlie periodic financial statements. Examples explained in this glossary are Accruals, Consistency, Going Concern, Objectivity, Prudence and Substance over Form.

ACCOUNTING IDENTITY (or EQUATION): Another name for the Balance Sheet Identity (q.v.).

ACCOUNTING PERIOD: The period between two balance sheets, usually a year from the point of view of shareholders and taxation authorities. Corporation tax is assessed on the basis of a company's accounting period.

ACCOUNTING POLICIES: The accounting methods selected and consistently followed by a business enterprise. Most companies publish a list of accounting policies in their annual reports.

ACCOUNTING REFERENCE PERIOD: A company's accounting

period as notified to the Registrar of Companies (31 March applies if notification is not given).

ACCOUNTING STANDARDS: *see* Statements of Standard Accounting Practice.

ACCOUNTING STANDARDS COMMITTEE (ASC): A committee established by the major professional accountancy bodies in the UK and Ireland to issue Statements of Standard Accounting Practice (q.v.).

ACCOUNTS PAYABLE: Amounts owing by a company; usually called creditors in Britain.

ACCOUNTS RECEIVABLE: Amounts owing to a company; usually called debtors in Britain.

ACCRUALS: The accounting concept that revenues are recognized as they are earned or incurred, not as money is received (accruals basis of accounting as distinct from cash basis).

ACCUMULATED DEPRECIATION: The cumulative amount of depreciation written off a fixed asset at a balance sheet date.

ACID TEST: Another name for the Liquid Ratio (q.v.).

ADVANCE CORPORATION TAX (ACT): Tax payable in advance when a company pays a dividend; the amount is tied to the basic rate of income tax. ACT is normally recoverable. The difference between the total corporation tax liability and ACT is known as Mainstream Corporation Tax (q.v.).

AKTIENGESELLSCHAFT (AG): The approximate German equivalent of the British public company.

ALLOTMENT: The allocation of shares by the directors of a company following applications for them by intending shareholders.

ALTERNATIVE ACCOUNTING RULES: The rules set out in the Companies Act allowing the application to company financial statements of accounting valuations based on current cost.

AMORTIZATION: The writing off over a period of an asset or a liability. Sometimes used synonymously with Depreciation (q.v.).

ANNUAL GENERAL MEETING (AGM): Meeting of the members (shareholders) of a company held annually at intervals of not more than fifteen months (but first AGM may be held within eighteen months of formation). Usual business transacted: reception of directors' report and accounts; declaration of dividend; election of directors; appointment of auditors.

ANNUAL REPORT: Report made annually by the directors of a company to its shareholders. Its contents are largely determined by company law and statements of standard accounting practice.

ANNUAL RETURN: Document which must be completed within forty-two days of the Annual General Meeting (q.v.) and forthwith forwarded to the Registrar of Companies (q.v.). Main contents are:

1. Address of registered office.
2. Addresses where registers of members and debenture-holders are kept.
3. Summary of share capital and debentures, giving number of issued shares of each class, the consideration for them, details of shares not fully paid-up, etc.
4. Particulars of mortgages and charges.
5. List of names and addresses of past and present shareholders giving number of shares held and particulars of transfers.
6. Names, addresses and occupations of directors and secretaries (and nationality of directors).

Copies of the financial statements, directors' report and auditors' report must be annexed to the return.

All the above can be inspected at the Companies Registries in Cardiff or Edinburgh on payment of a fee.

APPLICATION MONEY: The amount per share or unit of stock payable on application for a new issue of shares or debentures.

ARTICLES OF ASSOCIATION: The internal regulations of a company. They usually deal with: rights of various classes of shares; calls on shares; transfer, transmission and forfeiture of shares; alteration of share capital; general meetings (notice, proceedings); votes and proxies; directors (powers, duties, disqualification, rotation, proceedings); dividends and reserves; accounts; capitalization of profits; audit; winding up; and similar matters.

ASSET: Any property tangible or intangible from which future benefits are expected, and of which a company has a legal right of use as a result of a past or present transaction. Examples include machinery, stock-in-trade, debtors, cash, goodwill.

ASSOCIATED COMPANY: A company over which an investing group or company has a significant influence and in which the investor is *either* a partner in a joint venture or consortium *or* has a long-term and substantial interest.

AUDITORS: Independent experts who report to the shareholders of a company their opinion on the truth and fairness of published financial statements. Their remuneration (including expenses) must be disclosed in the published profit and loss account.

Auditors must either be members of a body of accountants established in the UK and recognized by the Department of Trade and Industry, or be authorized by the Department to be appointed. The auditor must not be an officer or servant of the company or of a company in the group; a body corporate; or a partner or employee of an officer or servant of the company or a company in the group.

AUTHORIZED SHARE CAPITAL: The maximum share capital which the directors of a company can issue at any given time. Disclosed in the balance sheet or the notes. The authorized minimum share capital of a public company is at present £50,000.

AVERAGE COLLECTION PERIOD: The speed at which a company collects its debts:

$$\frac{\text{debtors} \times 365}{\text{credit sales}} \text{ days}$$

BAD DEBT: An amount owing which is not expected to be received. It is written off either direct to profit and loss account or by way of a previously established provision for bad (or doubtful) debts.

BALANCE SHEET: Statement of the assets, liabilities and shareholders' funds of a company at a particular date. The Companies Act prescribes a choice of two balance sheet formats and that every balance sheet shall give a true and fair view of the state of affairs of the company.

BALANCE SHEET IDENTITY (or EQUATION): The identity: assets *equals* liabilities *plus* shareholders' funds.

BEARER SECURITIES: Debentures or shares transferable by simple delivery.

BETA: A measure of the market (or systematic) risk of a company's shares (i.e., the sensitivity of the share price to movements in the market).

BIG EIGHT: The eight largest public accountancy firms worldwide.

BONDS: Fixed interest securities such as government loans or (in the USA) company debentures.

BONUS SHARES: Shares issued to existing shareholders without further payment on their part. Also referred to as a scrip issue, a capitalization issue and (in the USA) a stock dividend.

BOOK VALUE: The monetary amount of an asset as stated in the balance sheet and books of account.

CALLED-UP SHARE CAPITAL: The amount of the Issued Share Capital (q.v.) which has been called up (i.e., the amounts shareholders have been asked to pay to date). Equal to the paid-up share capital unless there are calls in arrears or calls have been paid in advance.

CALLS: Demands by a company for part or all of the balance owed on partly paid shares.

CAPITAL ALLOWANCES: In effect, the depreciation allowable for tax purposes. At times it has differed quite substantially from that charged in the published financial statements.

CAPITAL EMPLOYED: Usually refers to the total of shareholders' funds plus long-term debt, but may be used to refer to fixed assets plus net current assets.

CAPITAL EXPENDITURE: Expenditure on fixed assets. The amount of contracts for capital expenditure not provided for and the amount of capital expenditure authorized by the directors but not contracted for must be disclosed.

CAPITAL GAINS TAX: A tax on individuals. Companies pay corporation tax on their capital gains, not capital gains tax.

CAPITAL REDEMPTION RESERVE: When shares are redeemed otherwise than out of a new issue of shares, a sum equal to their nominal value must be transferred to an account with this name. For most purposes the reserve is treated as if it were Share Capital (q.v.).

CAPITAL STRUCTURE: The composition of a company's sources of funds, especially long-term.

CAPITALIZATION ISSUE: *see* Bonus Issue.

CASH BUDGET: A plan of future cash receipts and payments based on specified assumptions concerning sales growth, credit terms, etc.

CASH FLOW: An imprecise term; usually defined as net profit plus depreciation and other items not involving the movement of funds (i.e., total funds generated from operations). Not the same as the change in cash balance during the year.

CHAIRMAN'S REVIEW (or STATEMENT): Statement made by the chairman of a company at its annual general meeting and often included in the annual report. There are no legal regulations relating to its contents, but it often contains interesting and useful information.

CLOSE COMPANY: A company resident in the UK which is under the control of five or fewer participators, or of participators who are directors. Introduced by the Finance Act 1965.

COMMON STOCK: American term for Ordinary Shares (q.v.).

COMPANY: Rather imprecise term implying corporate activity. This book deals with companies registered under the Companies Acts. The liability of such companies is limited (either by shares or by guarantee) except in the case of unlimited companies.

COMPARABILITY: An accounting concept which emphasizes ease of comparison of the financial statements of different companies at a point in time.

CONSERVATISM: *see* Prudence.

CONSISTENCY: An accounting concept which emphasizes consistency of Accounting Policies (q.v.) over time for a particular company rather than Comparability (q.v.) of the financial statements of different companies at any one point in time.

CONSOLIDATED BALANCE SHEET: Balance sheet of a group of companies as distinct from the holding company only.

CONSOLIDATED PROFIT AND LOSS ACCOUNT: Profit and loss account of a group of companies as distinct from the holding company only. A holding company need not publish its own profit and loss account as well if the consolidated profit and loss account discloses the requisite details (*see* Profit and Loss Account) and also discloses what portion of the consolidated profit (or loss) has been dealt with in its accounts.

CONSOLIDATION OF SHARE CAPITAL: Combination of shares into larger units (e.g., combining two 50p shares into one of £1).

CONTINGENCIES: Conditions which exist at the balance sheet date the outcome of which will be confirmed only on the occurrence or non-occurrence of one or more uncertain events. Contingent liabilities must be disclosed as a note to the balance sheet.

CONVERTIBLE LOAN STOCK: Loan stock which may be converted at the option of the holder at a future date or dates into ordinary stock at given price ratios.

COPYRIGHT: A right to published material.

CORPORATION TAX: A tax on companies; not payable by individuals. The rate may vary. There is a lower rate for small profits.

COST OF CAPITAL: The cost to a company of obtaining funds for investment.

COST OF SALES: The cost of goods sold during a period, calculated by adjusting cost of goods purchased or manufactured by the change in stocks.

COST OF SALES ADJUSTMENT (COSA): An adjustment made in Current Cost Accounting (q.v.) in order to base the cost of goods sold on the cost current at the time of consumption instead of the time of purchase.

COUPON RATE OF INTEREST: The rate of interest on the par value of a debenture or bond. Not necessarily equal to the effective rate.

CREDIT: *see* Double Entry.

CREDITORS: Amounts, representing either cash or a claim to services, owed to a company. A distinction is made between amounts falling due within one year (also known as Current Liabilities, q.v.) and amounts falling due after more than one year.

CUM: Latin for 'with'. A price so quoted includes any dividend (div.), bonus issue, rights or other distribution.

CUMULATIVE PREFERENCE SHARES: Preference shares entitled to be paid the arrears of their dividend before any dividend is paid on the ordinary shares. Any arrears must be disclosed in the notes.

CURRENT ASSET: Any asset other than a Fixed Asset (q.v.). Current assets are either already cash or can reasonably be expected to become cash within one year from the date of the balance sheet. Examples include debtors, stock-in-trade. If the directors believe that any of the current assets will not realize their balance-sheet values in the ordinary course of business, this fact must be disclosed. The alternative terms 'circulating assets' and 'floating assets' are obsolete.

CURRENT COST ACCOUNTING: A system of accounting in which assets are stated at the Value to the Business (q.v.) and current costs instead of historical costs are matched against revenues.

CURRENT LIABILITIES: Liabilities (q.v.) which are expected to have been paid within one year from the date of the balance sheet (e.g., trade creditors, proposed final dividend, current taxation).

CURRENT PURCHASING POWER (CPP) ACCOUNTING: A system of accounting which adjusts historical cost accounts for changes in the general price level.

CURRENT RATIO: Ratio of current assets to current liabilities. A measure of liquidity.

CURRENT TAXATION: Tax payable within one year from the date of the balance sheet.

DEBENTURE DISCOUNT: Arises from issuing debentures at less than their par value. Disclosed in balance sheet to the extent that it is not written off.

DEBENTURES: Loans, usually but not necessarily, secured on the assets of the company. Usually redeemable but may be irredeemable.

DEBIT: *see* Double Entry.

DEBTORS: Amounts owing to a company. They are classified for disclosure purposes into the following categories:

1. Trade debtors.

2. Amounts owed by group companies.
3. Amounts owed by related companies.
4. Other debtors.
5. Called-up share capital not paid.
6. Prepayments and accrued income.

Any amounts which fall due after more than one year must be shown separately for each category.

DEFENSIVE INTERVAL: A measure of how many days' operating expenses can be paid out of liquid assets.

DEFERRED ASSET: An asset representing cash receivable outside the forthcoming accounting period.

DEFERRED TAXATION: Taxation arising from timing differences between accounting profit and taxable income. The potential amount of deferred taxation payable is disclosed in the notes. Only deferred taxation which is reasonably probable to have to be paid within three years is included in the balance sheet.

DEPRECIATION: A measure of the wearing out, consumption or other loss of value of a fixed asset arising from use, effluxion of time or obsolescence through technology and market changes. Amount of depreciation charged must be disclosed. Usually measured by allocating either the historical or replacement cost less scrap value of the asset on a straight-line or reducing-balance basis. The accumulated (provision for) depreciation is deducted from the cost in the balance sheet to give the net book value. Depreciation is neither a source nor a use of funds.

DEPRECIATION ADJUSTMENT: An adjustment made in Current Cost Accounting (q.v.) in order to base depreciation on current replacement cost instead of historical cost.

DEPRIVAL VALUE: Synonym for Value to the Business (q.v.).

DILUTION: The decrease in control and/or earnings per share suffered by existing shareholders when a new issue of shares is wholly or partly subscribed to by new shareholders.

DIRECTIVE: A statement adopted by the Council of Ministers on the proposal of the Commission of the European Communities. Directives are implemented through national legislation.

DIRECTORS' EMOLUMENTS: The following information must be disclosed:

1. Aggregate amounts received by directors and past directors as emoluments, pensions and compensation in respect of services as directors and as executives.

2. Emoluments of chairman and of highest-paid director (if greater than chairman's).
3. Number of directors whose emoluments amounted to not more than £5,000, number whose emoluments amounted to between £5,001 and £10,000, and so on in bands of £5,000.
4. Number of directors who waived their emoluments and the aggregate amount waived.

   (Note: Points 2 and 3 do not apply to anyone whose duties were discharged wholly or mainly outside the UK. If the aggregate of directors' earnings does not exceed £60,000, no disclosure need be made thereof.)

DIRECTORS' REPORT: Annual report by the directors of a company to the shareholders which must disclose:

1. A fair review of the development of the business of the company and its subsidiaries during the financial year of their position at the end of it.
2. Proposed dividend.
3. Proposed transfers to reserves.
4. Names of directors.
5. Principal activities of the company and of its subsidiaries and any significant changes therein.
6. Significant changes in fixed assets of the company, or any of its subsidiaries.
7. An indication of the difference between the book and market values of land and buildings of the company, or any of its subsidiaries, if significant.
8. In relation to the company and its subsidiaries:
   (a) particulars of any important events which have occurred since the end of the financial year.
   (b) an indication of likely future developments in the business, and
   (c) an indication of any activities in the field of research and development.
9. Interests in shares or debentures of group companies of each person who was a director of the company at the end of the financial year (this may be given, instead, in the notes to the accounts).
10. Totals of UK political and charitable contributions of the company (or, if any made by subsidiaries, of the group), unless together not more than £200. The amount and name of political party or person paid for each contribution for political purposes over £200.

11. Where the company's average number of employees over the financial year exceeds 250, the company's policy as to:
    (a) employment of disabled persons.
    (b) continued employment and training of persons who become disabled while in the company's employment.
    (c) otherwise for the training, career development and promotion of disabled people.
12. Comprehensive particulars of the acquisition and disposal by a company of its own shares.

DISCOUNTED CASH FLOW: The present value of future cash receipts and payments (i.e., their value after taking into account the expected delay in receiving or paying them).

DISTRIBUTABLE RESERVES: A company's accumulated realized profits so far as not previously distributed or capitalized, *less* its accumulated realized losses so far as not previously written off in a reduction or reorganization of capital. Public companies may pay a dividend only if the net assets are not less than the aggregate of the called-up share capital and undistributable reserves.

DIVIDEND: That part of the profits of a company which is distributed to the shareholders. May be interim (paid during the financial year) or final (recommended by the directors for approval by the shareholders at the annual general meeting). The proposed final dividend is shown in the balance sheet as a current liability.

DIVIDEND CONTROL: Limitation of dividend payments by government regulation.

DIVIDEND COVER: The ratio between Earnings per Share (q.v.) and the ordinary dividend per share.

DIVIDEND POLICY: A company's policy on how to divide its profits between distributions to shareholders (dividends) and re-investment (retained profits).

DIVIDEND YIELD: The relationship between the ordinary dividend and the market price per ordinary share, usually multiplied by an appropriate fraction to allow for the Tax Credit (q.v.).

DOUBLE ENTRY: A system of recording transactions based on the Balance Sheet Identity (q.v.). Broadly, increases in assets and decreases in liabilities and capital items (including expenses) are *debits*, and increases in liabilities and capital items (including revenues) and decreases in assets are *credits*.

EARNINGS PER SHARE (EPS): Net profit attributable to the ordinary shareholder (before extraordinary items but after tax and preference dividends) divided by the weighted average number of ordinary shares. May be calculated on a Net, Nil or Maximum Basis (qq.v.). The 'basic' EPS may be supplemented by a 'fully diluted' EPS to allow for share options and convertible loan stock.

EARNINGS YIELD: The relationship between the earnings per ordinary share and the market price per ordinary share. The reciprocal of the Price–Earnings Ratio (q.v.) multiplied by 100.

EMPLOYEE INFORMATION: The following must be disclosed:

1. Total average number of employees and a division of this total by categories determined by the directors.
2. Staff costs divided into wages and salaries, social security costs, and other pension costs.
3. Number of employees in the UK whose emoluments exceeded £30,000, but were not more than £35,000, exceeded £35,000 but were not more than £40,000, and so on in bands of £5,000.

EMPLOYEE REPORT: A corporate financial report to employees, published either separately or as a supplement to a house magazine. Usually also made available to shareholders and other interested parties. Often includes a Value Added Statement (q.v.).

EQUITY METHOD: Method of accounting for investments in associated companies.

EQUITY SHARE CAPITAL: Defined by the Companies Acts as any issued share capital which has unlimited rights to participate in either the distribution of dividends or capital. Often more narrowly defined to mean Ordinary Shares (q.v.) only.

EX: Latin for 'without'. A price so quoted excludes any dividend (div.), bonus issue, rights or other distribution.

EXCEPTIONAL ITEMS: Items exceptional on account of size and/or incidence which derive from the ordinary activities of a business. Compare Extraordinary Items.

EXEMPT PRIVATE COMPANY: No longer exists. Before the Companies Act 1967 it was essentially a family company with the privilege of not having to publish its financial statements.

EXPOSURE DRAFT: A draft Statement of Standard Accounting Practice (q.v.) published for comment by interested parties.

EXTRAORDINARY ITEMS: Items which derive from events or transactions outside the ordinary activities of a business and which are both material and expected not to recur frequently or regularly. Compare Exceptional Items.

FINANCIAL RATIO: Relationship among items in financial statements.

FINANCIAL STATEMENTS: Statements showing the financial position (balance sheet), profit for a period (profit and loss account), and sources and uses of funds for a period (source and application of funds statement) of a company. Some companies also publish a statement of value added.

FINANCIAL YEAR: Runs for corporation tax purposes from 1 April to the following 31 March.

FIXED ASSETS: Those assets which are intended for use on a continuing basis in an undertaking's activities. Divided into Intangible Fixed Assets and Tangible Fixed Assets (qq.v.).

FIXED CHARGE: A charge which is attached to some specific asset or assets.

FIXED OVERHEADS: Those overheads whose amount remains constant over the usual range of activity.

FLAT YIELD: A Yield (q.v.) which does not take account of the redemption value of a security.

FLOATING CHARGE: A charge which is not attached to any specific asset but to all assets or to a class of assets.

FOREIGN COMPANY: A company incorporated outside Great Britain.

FOREIGN CURRENCIES: The financial statements of foreign subsidiaries must be translated into sterling before they can be included in the consolidated statements. The method of translation, of which the most common is the 'closing rate method', must be disclosed.

FRANKED INVESTMENT INCOME: Dividends received by one British company from another, with the addition of the related tax credit. The dividend and the credit can be passed on to the shareholders of the recipient company without payment of corporation tax.

FUNDS STATEMENT: *see* Source and Application of Funds, Statement of.

GEARING: The relationship between the funds provided to a company by its ordinary shareholders and the long-term sources of funds carrying a fixed interest charge or dividend.

GEARING ADJUSTMENT: An adjustment in current cost accounts intended to show the benefit to shareholders of the use of long-term debt, measured by the extent to which the net operating assets are financed by borrowing.

GESELLSCHAFT MIT BESCHRÄNKTER HAFTUNG (GmbH): The approximate German equivalent of the British private company.

GOING CONCERN: An accounting concept which assumes that an enterprise will continue in operational existence for the foreseeable future.

GOODWILL: The difference between the value of a company as a whole and the algebraic sum of the values of the assets and liabilities taken separately. Recorded only when purchased. Purchased goodwill is either written off immediately to reserves or amortized through the profit and loss account over its economic life.

GOODWILL ON CONSOLIDATION: The excess of the cost of shares in subsidiary companies over the book value of their net tangible assets at the date of acquisition. Can only appear in a *consolidated* balance sheet.

GROSS PROFIT: The excess of sales over costs of sales.

GROUP ACCOUNTS: Financial statements of a group of companies as distinct from the holding company only. The Companies Act provides that they are to be submitted if a company has subsidiary companies and is not a wholly owned subsidiary of another company incorporated in Great Britain.

GUARANTEE, COMPANY LIMITED BY: A company the liability of whose members is limited to contributing a predetermined amount in the event of the company being wound up. Companies may be limited by guarantee or by shares, or be unlimited.

HARMONIZATION: The process of narrowing differences in accounting practices, especially among countries.

HISTORICAL COST: The traditional basis of valuation in published financial statements. Often modified in the UK by the revaluation of land and buildings. Favoured because it is more objective and more easily verifiable by an auditor.

HISTORICAL COST ACCOUNTING RULES: The rules set out in the Companies Act requiring the application to company financial statements of accounting valuations based on historical cost. Companies must follow either these rules or the Alternative Accounting Rules (q.v.).

HOLDING COMPANY: Company which controls another company, called its subsidiary. Balance sheet of holding company must show separately shares (including basis of valuation) and amounts owing to and owed by subsidiaries.

IMPUTATION SYSTEM: System of corporate taxation under which all or part of the tax paid on distributed profits by the company is credited to the shareholders, thus mitigating double taxation.

INCOME STATEMENT: American term for Profit and Loss Account (q.v.).

INCOME TAX: A tax on individuals not payable by companies. The basic rate of income tax varies.

INDUSTRY RATIO: An average ratio for an industry.

INFLATION ACCOUNTING: System of accounting which allows for changes in general and/or specific prices. *See also* Current Cost Accounting *and* Current Purchasing Power Accounting.

INITIAL ALLOWANCE: Allowance for tax purposes given in the first year of life. Unlike an Investment Allowance (q.v.), it restricts the amount of the Writing-Down Allowances (q.v.) also given.

INSOLVENCY: An inability to pay debts as they fall due.

INSTITUTIONAL SHAREHOLDERS: Shareholders other than persons, industrial and commercial companies, the public sector and the overseas sector (i.e., financial institutions such as insurance companies and pension funds). Of increasing importance.

INTANGIBLE FIXED ASSETS: Assets such as Goodwill, Patents, Trade Marks and Copyrights (qq.v.) which have no tangible form.

INTERIM DIVIDEND: *see* Dividend.

INTERIM REPORT: Report issued by a company to its shareholders during a financial year (e.g., quarterly, half-yearly).

INVENTORIES: American term for stock-in-trade.

INVESTMENT ALLOWANCE: Allowance for tax purposes formerly given in first year of life of some fixed assets. Unlike an Initial Allowance (q.v.), it did not restrict the amount of the Writing-Down Allowances (q.v.) also given. The total allowances granted were thus greater than the acquisition cost (less scrap value) of the asset.

INVESTMENTS: Shares, loans, bonds and debentures held either as fixed tangible assets or current assets. Listed investments must be distinguished from unlisted.

INVESTMENT TRUST: Not really a trust but a company whose object is investment in the securities of other companies. Compare Unit Trust.

IRREDEEMABLE DEBENTURE: A Debenture (q.v.) which will never have to be repaid.

ISSUED SHARE CAPITAL: The amount of the Authorized Share Capital (q.v.) which has been issued; the remainder is the unissued share capital. The amount of the issued capital must be disclosed in the Notes. Not necessarily equal to called-up or paid-up share capital.

ISSUE EXPENSES: Expenses of making an issue of shares or debentures. Disclosed in balance sheet to the extent that they are not written off.

ISSUE PRICE: The price at which a share or debenture is issued; not necessarily equal to the Par Value (q.v.).

LEASING: Entering into a long-term contract which allows the use of an asset in return for a periodic rental, but does not give ownership. Its effect is similar to financing the purchase of the asset by loan capital.

LEVERAGE: The American term for Gearing (q.v.).

LIABILITIES: Amounts owing by a company. They are classified for disclosure purposes into the following categories:

1. Debenture loans.
2. Bank loans and overdrafts.
3. Payments received on account.
4. Trade creditors.
5. Bills of exchange payable.
6. Amounts owed to group companies.
7. Amounts owed to related companies.
8. Other creditors including taxation and social security.
9. Accruals and deferred income.

For each item which is payable wholly or partly after five years from the balance-sheet date, there must be stated:

1. The aggregate amount payable otherwise than by instalments.
2. The aggregate amount payable by instalments, and the aggregate amount of instalments which fall due after five years.
3. The terms of payment and rates of interest payable.

There must also be stated for each heading the aggregate amount of debts for which any security has been given and an indication of the nature of the security.

Listed companies are required by the stock exchange to show in addition, subdivided between bank loans and overdrafts and other borrowings, the aggregate amounts repayable:

1. In one year or less, or on demand.
2. Between one and two years.
3. Between two and five years.
4. In five years or more.

LIMITED LIABILITY COMPANY: A company the liability of whose members is limited by shares or by guarantee. If by shares, liability is limited to the amount taken up or agreed to be taken up; if by guarantee, to the amount undertaken to be contributed in the event of winding-up.

LIQUID ASSETS: Current assets *less* stock-in-trade.

LIQUID RATIO: The relationship between liquid assets and current liabilities. Also known as quick ratio, or the acid test.

LISTED COMPANY: A public company listed (quoted) on a recognized stock exchange.

LISTED INVESTMENTS: Investments which are listed on a recognized stock exchange or on any reputable stock exchange outside Great Britain. Must be shown separately in the balance sheet.

LOAN CAPITAL: Funds acquired by non-short-term borrowing from sources other than the shareholders of the company.

LONG-TERM DEBT: Long-term sources of funds other than equity (share capital and reserves).

MAINSTREAM CORPORATION TAX: The difference between a company's total liability to corporation tax and advance corporation tax.

MARKET PRICE: The price at which a company's securities can be bought or sold on a stock exchange. Not necessarily equal to the Par Value or the Issue Price (qq.v.).

MATERIALITY: An accounting concept that requires disclosure only of data that are significant enough to be relevant to the needs of a potential user.

MAXIMUM BASIS: Method of calculating Earnings Per Share (q.v.) based on the assumption that a company distributes all its profits and is liable to pay advance corporation tax on them.

MEDIUM COMPANIES: Companies with the privilege of filing modified profit and loss accounts and notes with the Registrar of Companies. 'Medium' is measured in terms of total assets, turnover and average number of employees.

MEMORANDUM OF ASSOCIATION: A document which states:

1. The name of the company.
2. That the company is a public company (if such is the case).
3. The situation of the registered office.
4. The objects of the company.
5. That the liability of the members is limited (unless the company is an unlimited one).
6. The authorized share capital and how it is divided (or, in the case of a company limited by guarantee, the maximum amount to be contributed by members on winding-up).

7. Details of the subscribers (the persons 'desirous of being formed into a company').

MERGER ACCOUNTING: A system of accounting which assumes the merger of two or more companies rather than the takeover of one by another.

MINORITY INTEREST: That part of a subsidiary company's shareholders' funds that is not held by the holding company. Usually shown as a separate item on the capital and liabilities side of a consolidated balance sheet.

MONETARY WORKING CAPITAL ADJUSTMENT (MWCA): An adjustment made in current cost accounting in order to take account of the effect of increased prices on monetary working capital (bank balances + debtors − creditors).

NET BASIS: Method of calculating Earnings Per Share (q.v.) which takes account of both constant and variable components in the tax charge.

NET CURRENT ASSETS: Another name for Working Capital (q.v.).

NET PROFIT: The excess of revenues over expenses. Calculated before or after extraordinary items and before or after tax depending upon the context.

NET PROFIT RATIO: Ratio of net profit to sales.

NET REALIZABLE VALUE: The amount for which an asset can be sold, net of the expenses of sale.

NET TANGIBLE ASSETS: Assets except for intangible assets *less* liabilities.

NET WORKING CAPITAL: Another name for Working Capital (q.v.).

NIL BASIS: Method of calculating Earnings Per Share (q.v.) which assumes a nil distribution of dividends.

NO CREDIT INTERVAL: Another term for Defensive Interval (q.v.).

NOMINEE SHAREHOLDER: A shareholder who holds shares on behalf of another person or company who is the beneficial shareholder.

NOMINAL SHARE CAPITAL: *see* Authorized Share Capital.

NON-MONETARY ASSETS: Assets other than monetary assets (i.e., mainly fixed assets and stock-in-trade).

NON-VOTING SHARES: Shares with no voting rights. Non-voting ordinary shares are usually cheaper to buy than those carrying votes. Often called 'A' shares.

NO PAR VALUE SHARES: Shares with no nominal or par value. They are illegal in Britain.

NOTES TO THE ACCOUNTS: Notes attached to and explanatory of items in the financial statements. May be very detailed.

OBJECTIVITY: Accounting concept which stresses the need to establish rules for recording financial transactions and events which so far as possible do not depend upon the personal judgement of the recorder.

OFF BALANCE SHEET FINANCING: Financing assets by 'borrowing' in such a fashion that the debt does not appear as a balance sheet item.

ORDINARY SHARES: Shares entitled to share in the profits after payment of debenture interest and preference dividends. Often referred to as the equity capital.

OVERHEADS: Expenses other than the direct costs of material and labour.

OVERTRADING: A situation in which a company expands its sales and may appear to be highly profitable but does not have the resources available to finance the expansion and is therefore in danger of running out of cash.

PAID-UP SHARE CAPITAL: The amount of the Called-Up Share Capital (q.v.) which has been paid up by the shareholders.

PARENT COMPANY: *see* Holding Company.

PAR VALUE: The face or nominal value of a share or debenture. Not necessarily equal to the Issue Price or the current Market Price (qq.v.). Dividend and interest percentages refer to the par value, Yields (q.v.) to the current market price.

PATENTS: Grants by the Crown to the authors of new inventions giving them the sole and exclusive right to use, exercise and sell their inventions and to secure the profits arising therefrom for a limited period.

POST BALANCE SHEET EVENTS: Events occurring after the date of the balance sheet. They are either 'adjusting events' (those providing additional evidence of conditions existing at the balance-sheet date) or 'non-adjusting events'.

PRE-ACQUISITION PROFITS: The accumulated profits of a subsidiary company up to the date of its acquisition (take-over) by the holding company.

PREFERENCE SHARES: Shares which usually are entitled to a fixed rate of dividend before a dividend is paid on the ordinary shares and to priority of repayment if the company is wound up. Participating preference shares are also entitled to a further dividend if profits are available. If a preference dividend is not paid, the arrears must be disclosed as a note to the balance sheet. Arrears can only arise if the shares are *cumulative* as distinct from *non-cumulative*.

PRELIMINARY EXPENSES. Expenses of forming a company.

PRICE-EARNINGS RATIO: The multiple of the last reported Earnings Per Share (q.v.) that the market is willing to pay per ordinary share. The reciprocal of the Earnings Yield (q.v.) multiplied by 100.

PRIOR CHARGES: Claims on a company's assets and profits that rank ahead of ordinary share capital.

PRIORITY PERCENTAGES: Method of calculating Gearing (q.v.) by computing the percentage of earnings that is required to service each category of loan and share capital.

PRIOR YEAR ADJUSTMENTS: Material adjustments applicable to prior years arising from changes in accounting policies or from the correction of fundamental errors.

PRIVATE COMPANY: A company which is not a Public Company (q.v.). Not permitted to issue shares or debentures to the public.

PROFIT: A general term for the excess of revenues over expenses. *See* Gross Profit and Net Profit.

PROFIT AND LOSS ACCOUNT: Statement of the revenue, expenses and profit of a company for a particular period. The Companies Act prescribes a choice of four profit and loss account formats and that every profit and loss account shall give a true and fair view of the profit or loss for the financial year. A published profit and loss account includes appropriations of profit and is therefore a combination of a profit and loss account proper and a profit and loss appropriation account.

PROFIT AND LOSS APPROPRIATION ACCOUNT: Continuation of profit and loss account proper giving details of profit appropriations (i.e., distribution as dividends and retention as reserves).

PROSPECTUS: Any notice, circular, advertisement or other invitation offering share or debentures to the public.

PROVISION: Either a Provision for Liabilities and Charges (q.v.) or a valuation adjustment, i.e., an amount written off fixed assets (by way of depreciation or amortization) or current assets (e.g., a provision for doubtful debts). In both cases a charge is made to profit and loss account, but Provisions for Liabilities and Charges are shown in the balance sheet as part of the capital and liabilities, whereas valuation adjustments are deducted from the asset concerned.

PROVISION FOR LIABILITIES AND CHARGES: Amount retained as reasonably necessary for the purpose of providing for any liability or loss which is either likely to be incurred, or certain to be incurred, but uncertain as to the amount or as to the date on which it will arise. Examples include pensions and deferred taxation.

PROXY:

1. A person appointed to attend and vote at a company meeting on behalf of a shareholder.
2. The form, signed by the shareholder, which grants the above authority.

PRUDENCE: Accounting concept under which revenue and profits are not anticipated but are recognized by inclusion in the profit and loss account only when realized in cash or other assets, the ultimate realization of which can be assessed with reasonable certainty. Provision is made for all known liabilities, whether the amount of these is known with certainty or is a best estimate in the light of the information available.

PUBLIC COMPANY: A company whose Memorandum of Association (q.v.) states that it is a public company, whose name ends with the words 'public limited company' (plc; ccc for Welsh companies) and which has a minimum authorized and allotted share capital at least one quarter paid up.

QUICK ASSETS: Current assets *less* stock-in-trade.
QUICK RATIO: *See* Liquid Ratio.

RECOVERABLE AMOUNT: The greater of the Net Realizable Value (q.v.) of an asset and the amount recoverable from its further use.
REDEEMABLE SHARES: Shares which must or may be redeemed at the option of the company or (very rarely) the shareholder. The balance sheet must disclose the earliest and latest dates on which the company has power to redeem, whether at the option of the company or in any event, and also the amount of any premium on redemption.
REDEMPTION YIELD: A Yield (q.v.) which takes into account not only the annual interest receivable but also the redemption value of a security.
REDUCING BALANCE DEPRECIATION: Method of depreciation in which the periodic amount written off decreases over the life of the asset. A fixed percentage is applied to a declining written-down value.
REGISTERED OFFICE: The official address of a company. The Mem-

orandum of Association (q.v.) must state whether it is in England and Wales, or in Scotland.

REGISTRAR OF COMPANIES: Government officer with whom annual reports (including financial statements) and other documents must be filed; in Cardiff for companies registered in England and Wales, in Edinburgh for companies registered in Scotland.

RELATED COMPANIES: Term used in the Companies Act for what is essentially an Associated Company (q.v.).

REPLACEMENT COST: The cost of replacing an asset.

RESEARCH AND DEVELOPMENT EXPENDITURE: Includes expenditure on pure research, applied research and development. Only the last is in some circumstances treated as an asset.

RESERVE: Reserves arise either from the retention of profits or from events such as the issue of shares at a premium or the revaluation of assets. Must not include Provisions (q.v.) unless the directors consider the latter are excessive. Not a charge against profits and not usually represented by cash on the other side of the balance sheet. Movements in reserves during the financial year must be disclosed.

RESERVE FUND: A Reserve (q.v.) which is represented by specially earmarked cash or investments on the other side of the balance sheet.

RETAINED PROFITS: Profits not distributed to shareholders but re-invested in the company. Their cost is less than a new issue of shares, because of the issue costs of the latter.

RETURN ON INVESTMENT: Ratio of profit (usually before interest and tax) to net tangible assets. A measure of profitability.

REVALUATION: The writing-up of an asset to its current market value.

REVALUATION RESERVE: The amount of profit or loss arising from the revaluation of any asset. An undistributable reserve unless the profit or loss has been realized.

REVENUE EXPENDITURE: Expenditure that is written off completely in the profit and loss account in the accounting period in which it is made.

REVERSE YIELD GAP: A description of the fact that since August 1959 the average yield on government bonds has been greater than the average dividend yield on the ordinary shares of companies, despite the greater (monetary) security of the former.

RIGHTS ISSUE: An issue of shares in which the existing shareholders have a right to subscribe for the new shares at a stated price. The right can be sold if the shareholder does not wish to subscribe.

RISK: Of two kinds: Systematic (or market) risk and Specific (or non-market) risk (qq.v.).

SALE-AND-LEASEBACK: Raising cash by selling an asset and then leasing it back in a long-term contract. *See also* Leasing.

SCRAP VALUE: The amount at which a fixed asset is expected to be sold at the end of its estimated economic life.

SCRIP ISSUE: *See* Bonus Shares.

SECURITIES AND EXCHANGE COMMISSION (SEC): American federal body concerned with the operations of corporations (i.e., companies) and issues of and dealings in their securities. It has the right, which it has largely delegated to the Financial Accounting Standards Board, to establish accounting principles.

SECURITY: Two meanings:

1. A generic name for stocks, shares, debentures, etc.
2. The backing for a loan.

SEGMENT REPORTING: Reporting the results of a diversified group of companies by major class of business and geographical area. The Companies Act requires disclosure in the notes of turnover and profit or loss before taxation attributable to each class of business that, in the opinion of the directors, differs substantially from any other class. Turnover must also be disclosed by geographical markets where, in the opinion of the directors, these differ substantially from each other. A geographical analysis of turnover is also required by the stock exchange.

SHARE CAPITAL: Unless limited by guarantee, a company registered under the Companies Acts must have a share capital divided into shares of a fixed amount. The ownership of a share gives the shareholder a proportionate ownership of the company. The share capital is stated in the balance sheet at its par (nominal) value.

SHAREHOLDER: Member of a company whose part ownership of (share in) the company is evidenced by a share certificate.

SHAREHOLDERS' FUNDS: The proprietorship section of a company balance sheet. Includes the share capital and the reserves.

SHARE OPTION: The right to buy or sell shares within a stated period.

SHARE PREMIUM: Results from issuing shares at a price higher than their par value. Must be disclosed in the balance sheet as a Reserve (q.v.). Cannot be used to pay dividends but can be used to make an issue of Bonus Shares (q.v.).

SMALL COMPANIES: Companies with the privilege of filing with the Registrar of Companies a modified balance sheet and notes and omitting from filing a profit and loss account and directors' report 'Small' is measured in terms of total assets, turnover and average number of employees.

SMALL COMPANIES RELIEF: A reduced rate of corporation tax paid by companies with small taxable incomes. This tax relief is not related to small companies as defined in the Companies Act.

SOCIÉTÉ ANONYME (SA): The approximate French equivalent of a British public company.

SOCIÉTÉ À RESPONSABILITÉ LIMITÉE (SARL): The approximate French equivalent of a British private company.

SOLVENCY: The ability of a debtor to pay debts as they fall due.

SOURCE AND APPLICATION OF FUNDS, STATEMENT OF: A statement showing the sources of funds (e.g., new issue of shares or debentures, retained profits) and the uses of funds (e.g., purchase of new fixed assets, increase in working capital) of a company over a period.

SPECIFIC PRICES: The prices, observable in a market, of specific goods and services. The government provides specific price indices periodically in its publication *Price Index Numbers for Current Cost Accounting*.

SPECIFIC RISK: Risk arising from factors specific to a company and not from the market generally.

STATEMENTS OF RECOMMENDED PRACTICE (SORPs): Non-mandatory statements approved by the Accounting Standards Committee.

STATEMENTS OF STANDARD ACCOUNTING PRACTICE (SSAPs): Statements of methods of accounting prepared by the Accounting Standards Committee and approved by the councils of the major professional accountancy bodies. They apply to all financial statements intended to give a true and fair view.

STOCK DIVIDEND: *See* Bonus Shares.

STOCK EXCHANGE: A market where shares, debentures, government securities, etc. are bought and sold. The London stock exchange is by far the largest in Britain; it is federated with the provincial exchanges.

STOCKS AND WORK IN PROGRESS: Comprises goods or other assets purchased for resale; consumable stores; raw materials and components; products and services in intermediate stages of completion; and finished goods. Valued at the lower of cost (historical cost under historical cost accounting; replacement cost under current cost accounting) or net realizable value.

STOCK TURNOVER: Ratio of sales (sometimes, cost of sales) to stock-in-trade.

STRAIGHT-LINE DEPRECIATION: Obtained by dividing the cost less estimated scrap value of an asset by its estimated economic life.

SUBDIVISION OF SHARE CAPITAL: Splitting of shares into smaller units (e.g., splitting one £1 share into two of 50p).

SUBSIDIARY: Company controlled by another company called its holding company. A company is a subsidiary of another company if that other company:

1. Is a member of it; and either
2. controls the composition of its board of directors; or
3. holds more than half the nominal value of its Equity Share Capital (q.v.).

SUBSTANCE OVER FORM: An accounting concept whereby transactions or other events are accounted for and presented in accordance with their economic substance rather than their legal form.

SYSTEMATIC (MARKET) RISK: Risk arising from the market, not from specific factors applicable to a company. Quantified as the beta of a company's ordinary shares.

TABLE A: A model set of Articles of Association (q.v.) which can be adopted by a company in full or in a modified form.

TAKE-OVER BID: An offer to purchase the share capital of a company.

TANGIBLE FIXED ASSETS: Assets such as land and buildings, plant and machinery, and fixtures and fittings.

TAXABLE INCOME: Income liable to tax. Not usually equal to the profit reported in a company's financial statements.

TAX CREDIT: A credit received by shareholders at the same time as a dividend. Its amount depends on the basic rate of income tax. It can be set off against the liability to income tax on the dividend plus tax credit.

TIMES INTEREST EARNED: The number of times that a company's interest is covered or earned by its profit before interest and tax.

TRADE CREDIT: Short-term source of funds resulting from credit granted by suppliers of goods bought.

TRADE DISCOUNT: A discount off the list price of a good. Sales and purchases are recorded net of trade discounts.

TRADE MARK: A distinctive identification, protected by law, of a manufactured product or of a service.

TRADING ON THE EQUITY: American expression describing the process of using fixed-interest sources of capital to boost the return on the equity (ordinary shares).

TRUE AND FAIR VIEW: The overriding reporting requirement for companies. The phrase is undefined but depends upon both the application of accounting standards and the exercise of judgement. If financial statements and the notes thereto do not in themselves give a true and fair view, additional information must be provided. In special circumstances the express requirements of the law must be departed from if this is necessary in order to give a true and fair view. A true and fair view is required, not *the* true and fair view.

TURNOVER: Sales, i.e., the amounts derived from the provision of goods and services falling within a company's ordinary activities after deduction of trade discounts, V A T and similar taxes. In consolidated financial statements it excludes inter-company transactions. *See also* Segment Reporting.

ULTRA VIRES: Latin for 'beyond the powers'. Especially applied to acts of a company not authorized by the objects clause of its memorandum of association.

UNDISTRIBUTABLE RESERVES: The aggregate of: share premium account; capital redemption reserve; accumulated unrealized profits, so far as not previously capitalized, *less* accumulated, unrealized losses, so far as not previously written off in a reduction or reorganization of capital; and other reserves a company is prohibited from distributing.

UNIT TRUST: Undertaking formed to invest in securities (mainly ordinary shares) under the terms of a trust deed. Not a company. Compare Investment Trust.

UNLIMITED COMPANY: A Company (q.v.) the liability of whose members is limited neither by shares nor by guarantee.

UNLISTED INVESTMENTS: Investments which are not listed on a recognized British stock exchange or on any reputable stock exchange outside Great Britain. If they consist of equity of other companies, directors must give either an estimate of their value or information about income received, profits, etc.

UNLISTED SECURITIES MARKET (USM): A separate market for companies not large enough to be listed upon the stock exchange. It imposes less stringent regulations.

UNSECURED LOAN: Money borrowed by a company without the giving of security.

VALUE ADDED STATEMENTS: A statement showing for a period the wealth created (value added) by the operations of an enterprise and how the wealth has been distributed among employees, government, providers of capital and replacement and expansion.

VALUE ADDED TAX (VAT): A tax based on the value added as goods pass from supplier of raw materials, to manufacturer, to wholesaler, to retailer, to consumer. Tax receivable can be set off against tax payable. Turnover is shown net of VAT in published profit and loss accounts.

VALUE TO THE BUSINESS: The deprival value of an asset, i.e., the lower of its current replacement cost and Recoverable Amount (q.v.). The basis of valuation in current cost accounting.

VARIABLE OVERHEADS: Overheads which vary proportionately with manufacturing activity.

WINDOW-DRESSING: The manipulation of figures in financial statements so as to produce a desired ratio on the balance-sheet date.

WORKING CAPITAL: Current assets *less* current liabilities.

WORK-IN-PROGRESS: Partly completed manufactured goods.

WRITING-DOWN ALLOWANCE: The annual amount deductible for tax purposes on certain tangible fixed assets.

WRITTEN-DOWN VALUE: The value of an asset in the books of a company or for tax purposes after depreciation has been written off.

YIELD: The rate of return relating cash invested to cash received (or expected to be received).

Z-SCORE: A measure of the Solvency of a company calculated from an equation incorporating more than one Financial Ratio (qq.v.).

Appendix C: Annual Report and Accounts of British Vita P L C for the Year Ended 31 December 1985

Preliminary announcement	
of results for year	Early March
Report and Accounts circulated	Late March
Annual General Meeting	Mid April
Interim Report	Early September

Dividend payments	
Interim	Mid November
Final	Mid May

Interest payments	
7¼% Debenture Stock	31 March, 30 September
10¼% Debenture Stock	30 June, 31 December

Financial Highlights

£000	1985	1984 (restated*)	1984
Turnover	186,108	133,950	138,391
Operating profit	11,790	7,824	9,528
Share of profit of associated companies	2,584	3,884	3,884
Profit on ordinary activities before taxation			
United Kingdom	4,476	4,548	4,430
Europe	4,726	1,513	1,513
International	3,029	4,387	5,908
	12,231	10,448	11,851
Profit for the year	3,717	5,686	6,363
Average capital employed	£62.4m	£56.8m	£56.9m
Return on capital employed	23%	21%	24%
Earnings per share	23.5p	22.0p	24.3p
Dividend per share	7.0p	6.2p	6.2p
Net assets per share	153p	169p	169p
Number of shares in issue	30.2m	30.1m	30.1m

*Reflecting change in basis of accounting for Zambian interests.

1

Directors

Chairman	F. A. Parker FCA, CBIM, FRSA*
Deputy chairman and chief executive	R. McGee FPRI
Directors	G. Blunt FBIM
	F. J. Eaton FPRI
	D. R. Hine BSc, CEng, MIChemE, AMCT
	L. D. Lawton BA, FRSA
	J. H. Ogden*
	R. H. Sellers BSc(Econ), FCA, DpBA
Secretary	A. R. Teague FCCA

Non-executive

Registered office	Soudan Street, Middleton, Manchester M24 2DB (Registered in England No. 871669)
Auditors	Arthur Andersen & Co., Chartered Accountants, 9 Charlotte Street, Manchester M1 4EU
Principal bankers	National Westminster Bank PLC
Registrars	National Westminster Bank PLC, Registrars Department, Bristol BS99 7NH

2

Notice of Meeting

Notice is hereby given that the Twentieth Annual General Meeting of British Vita PLC will be held at the Schoolhouse, Long Street, Middleton, Manchester on Wednesday 16 April 1986 at 2.15 pm for the following purposes:

Ordinary business

1 To receive and consider the accounts and the reports of the directors and auditors for the year ended 31 December 1985.

2 To confirm the dividends paid and to declare a final dividend on the Ordinary shares for the year ended 31 December 1985.

3 To re-elect Mr J. H. Ogden as a director.

4 To re-appoint Arthur Andersen & Co. as auditors of the Company and to authorise the directors to fix their remuneration.

Special business

5 To consider and if thought fit, pass the following resolution which will be proposed as a special resolution:

That in accordance with Section 95 of the Companies Act 1985 and in substitution of the authority contained in Article 8 of the Company's Articles of Association, the directors be and they are hereby empowered to allot equity securities (within the meaning of Section 94 of the Companies Act 1985) pursuant to the authority conferred by Resolution Number 6 passed at the Extraordinary General Meeting of the Company held on 25 October 1984 as if sub-section (i) of Section 89 of the Companies Act 1985 did not apply to any such allotment and the directors may at any time prior to the expiry of the power hereby conferred, or any renewal thereof, make any offer or agreement which would or might require equity securities to be allotted after such expiry and the directors may allot equity securities in pursuance of such offer or agreement accordingly provided that the power hereby granted shall unless renewed expire at the conclusion of the Twenty First Annual General Meeting of the Company and shall be limited:—

(i) to the allotment of equity securities in connection with a rights issue where it is reasonably necessary otherwise than in accordance with Section 89(i) of the Companies Act 1985;

(ii) to the allotment (otherwise than pursuant to paragraph (i) above) of equity securities up to an aggregate nominal amount of £475,000.

By order of the Board
A. R. Teague
Secretary

Soudan Street,
Middleton,
Manchester
24 March 1986   M24 2DB

An Ordinary shareholder entitled to attend and vote is entitled to appoint one or more proxies (whether members or not) to attend and, on a poll, vote instead of him. A form of proxy must reach the Company's Registrars, National Westminster Bank PLC by 2.15 pm on Monday 14 April 1986. A form of proxy is included for the use of Ordinary shareholders.

Copies of the directors' contracts of service and the rules of the Company's share option schemes will be available for inspection at the Registered Office of the Company on any weekday (Saturdays and public holidays excepted) during normal business hours and for a period of fifteen minutes prior to and during the meeting.

3

Chairman's Review

For the third successive year the Group has produced another increased level of profit, and this was achieved after excluding the pre-tax profits of the Group's Zambian interests which in 1984 amounted to £1,403,000. The pre-tax profit of £12.2m therefore is an increase of 17% over the restated profit for the previous year.

Results from two of the UK operations, consumer and textile, which have been undergoing restructuring, detracted from an otherwise good performance from the UK businesses. The European results include a full year for the French operations and those of the foam interests of the Solvay Group from July last, the date of their acquisition.

As I reported in my interim statement it was pleasing to conclude a major agreement providing for the manufacture under licence in North America of "Tramivex" car headliners. This technology has attracted considerable interest around the world and further

licences in other important car producing countries are expected to follow. Licensing income, including that from 150 licensees of the Maxfoam process for polyether manufacture established worldwide, particularly in the USA, will provide a growing proportion of the profit in the years ahead.

The continued development of the Group into Continental Europe with operations now in the Netherlands, France, Belgium, Germany and Switzerland is part fulfilment of the Board's strategy to improve the quality of the Group's net profits. By this I mean that an increasing percentage of those profits is arising in countries where dividends can be remitted to the UK without being subject to exchange control restrictions. The acquisition last July of the Solvay Group foam interests added to our already strong technological base and a committee of senior technologists is now charged with the cross fertilisation of this technical knowledge throughout the Group.

4

The international interests of the Group were the subject of some rationalisation during the year with some smaller units being sold off and others strengthened, in some instances with extension into other product lines. Foreign exchange factors have again proved to be a problem to the Group with movements in exchange rates affecting results significantly. Nevertheless the international operations continue to have long term growth prospects.

The accounts for 1985 reflect the decision of the Board to omit the results relating to the two very profitable Zambian subsidiaries. This is owing to the ongoing uncertainty surrounding the remission of profits from those subsidiaries due to the continuing shortage of foreign currency in Zambia. The Group will continue to support the two companies and indeed trade between them and the UK remains as before.

The major portion of the extraordinary items shown in the accounts is the loss on realising the assets representing the blocked funds in Zambia. Also included under the same heading are the costs incurred during the year in the restructuring of some, and the closure of other, businesses within the UK consumer and textile operations.

The Balance Sheet gearing at the year end was 42% against a forecast following the acquisitions of last July of over 50%. This reflects the good trading results and cash management in the second half of the year.

The Board is proposing a final dividend of 3.7p making a total for the year of 7p (1984 6.2p)—equivalent to 10p gross — thus showing its confidence for the future growth of the Group.

Personnel

During the year three directors resigned their membership of the Board, each for different reasons — Mr Norman Grimshaw to pursue his other interests, Mr Tom Richardson for early retirement and Mr William Holt to return to professional life. All served the Group well over many years both as managers and directors and I am sure you will, with me, wish them a successful future.

The opportunity has been taken to reorganise the central functions of the Group under Mr Rod Sellers, the financial director, who is now responsible for the corporate centre. I am pleased to welcome the new Group Secretary Mr Alan Teague who was formerly with the textile division. The performance of the Group personnel during the year can be seen from the results achieved and I take this opportunity of thanking them for their efforts in 1985 and I am confident of their contribution during the current year.

Future prospects

The year to date has seen a continuing good demand for the Group's products and there is every confidence for the rest of the year. This is applicable to both the UK operations and those in Continental Europe whilst internationally, subject to the movement of exchange rates, the overseas companies will increasingly contribute to the Group's growth.

The theme for 1986 is cash generation from the Group's enlarged business base but as is evident from the events of last year the Board will further its policy of Innovation, Investment and Growth as opportunities arise. The Board is planning for sustained growth in 1986 and beyond, based on existing products and operations, reinforced by new products developed from new technology and by acquisitions.

F. A. Parker

6 March 1986

5

Review of Operations

An analysis of turnover and profit, both by class of business and geographically, is shown on page 17 and examples of Group products, activities and trade names are given inside the back cover of this Report and Accounts. The following brief review summarises the significant events of the year in each of the Group's major operations.

United Kingdom Operations

Foams and Fibres — These divisions achieved satisfactory results overall in 1985 but fluctuations occurred during the year. The second quarter was weak due to a lack of demand from the domestic sector but this was balanced by strong demand towards the end of the year. Unfavourable exchange rates made exporting more difficult for much of the year.

Supplies of foam and fibre components for upholstery, bedding and apparel industries were maintained at good levels and the newer technical products for the computer, filtration and packaging industries made a very useful contribution. New plant for the production of reconstituted foam was commissioned early in the year and is performing well both in terms of quality of product and production efficiency.

Consumer products including quilts and pillows enjoyed high turnover but in highly competitive markets. However, recent diversifications into factoring bed linens and manufacturing pine bunk beds were not profitable and these operations ceased by the end of the year.

Good performance was achieved in the supplies of laminating foams and better efficiencies are now being obtained following the reorganisation and improvement of production facilities in late 1984. The operation is to be further reinforced with new handling and peeling equipment which will become operational by mid-1986.

1986 has started well with sales on or above budget. Although any fall in sterling against the deutsche mark could increase certain raw material prices, the broadening market and technical base of these operations should ensure that satisfactory progress continues to be made.

Fabrics and Polymers — The apparel, automotive and household textile markets served by the textile division experienced a variable demand throughout the year. The programme of closures and rationalisation continued in certain of the businesses and was aimed at achieving a more effective cost base. With emphasis on production efficiencies, product development and diversification, the division seeks to extend further its market outlets in 1986.

The industrial coated fabrics business improved consistently throughout the year, benefitting from ongoing development programmes and the improved requirements of the more traditional markets served.

Further progress was achieved in the polymer compounding operations during 1985 especially by introducing its compounding capability to a broader spread of industries and by improving export performance. The benefits of capital projects were evident in the adhesives and elastomers units. The commitment to increasing the range and scope of polymeric compounding expertise and service will be further reinforced with the opening of the division's extensive new research and development laboratory facilities early in 1986.

Demand in certain sectors of the polymer moulding business benefitted from the introduction of new vehicle models and increasing exports although other areas of the business remain static in the face of cost pressures in highly competitive market situations.

European Operations

The policy of expansion within Europe was significantly developed during 1985 with the acquisition of the foam interests of the Solvay Group in the Netherlands, Germany and Switzerland. In addition to its UK operations, the Group now has 17 manufacturing units strategically situated in five countries throughout Europe. These operations currently generate sales which are more than quadruple the levels attained by the Group's then existing European operations less than two years ago.

France — The acquisition of Tramico and Morard in July 1984 has proved most successful with the companies achieving good results in what was generally a falling market. Negotiations for the licensing of Tramico's "Tramivex" patented automotive trim components were concluded with the Van Dresser Corporation, the USA's leading manufacturer of automotive headliners. The agreement covers the next 15 years and Tramico has already supplied a plant to Van Dresser which should come on stream in mid-1986.

Considerable progress was made in 1985 in the sales of specialised protective foam used in military and security services clothing. This, together with other technical products, complements the foam and polymer components supplied to domestic markets for transportation, building, furniture and for general industrial uses.

6

Netherlands — After a difficult start to the year, the Group's foam operations in the Netherlands, which were significantly enlarged by the acquisition of Draka Interfoam and Veenendaal in mid-year, achieved good results with the new operations enabling a specialisation of activities to take place within the country. With strong market positions in the supplies of polyether foams in the domestic market especially for furniture and mattresses, the polyester foam operations are heavily orientated towards the export markets of Northern Europe.

Belgium — Libeltex achieved good results in 1985 and continues to be the largest fibre fillings processing operation in Europe serving not only the European but also significant export markets worldwide. The development of technically based products continues to have high priority and this brings a wide range of higher value added items into a broad industrial market.

Germany — The Group's first operations in Germany were acquired in mid-1985. There is an excellent geographical spread of production units with technically advanced plant at Oestrich near Frankfurt concentrating on polyester foams whilst high volume polyether foams for the furniture, bedding, packaging and automotive industries are produced in Bavaria and supplied from six conversion factories around the country. The companies operate in a highly competitive market place but efforts to bring profitability to proper levels are being assisted by the interchange of production know-how between all European Group Companies. Also benefits are expected to accrue from the improvements to the Oestrich site and plant which were carried out as part of the acquisition package from Solvay.

Other Countries — In addition to the Group's existing presence in Ireland where Vita Cortex supplies foam and fibre to its domestic packaging, furniture and apparel markets, Tramico is establishing a presence in Spain through a company licensed to produce "Tramivex" headliners for the growing Spanish automotive market.

Licensing of the widely used Maxfoam patented process for polyether foams is carried out by Unifoam in Switzerland.

International Operations
The results in 1985 were heavily influenced by the adverse impact of exchange rates on the translation of local currency results into sterling and also by the exclusion of the results of the Group's Zambian interests.

In the African operations, in spite of continuing difficulties in obtaining licences and foreign exchange for the importation of raw materials, most companies improved profits over previous years in local currency terms. The achievements of our Nigerian and Zambian management were particularly commendable and the overall performance was supported by good results from Kenya and Zimbabwe where new plant and equipment installed in late 1984 came into commercial production.

Expansion into synthetic fibre processing at a new industrial site in Egypt has been completed and the broader product range now available will complement the existing spread of foam and furniture products.

In Canada improvements came from most locations although in Ontario margins were affected by over capacity in a weak market. The Winnipeg operation was expanded late in the year whilst, in Montreal, the converting unit was moved into more suitable premises. The industrial, leisure and medicare products division showed excellent performance in its specialised market area.

The restricted market for our products in the Caribbean has caused us to review our involvement there and our equity in the Trinidad company is being sold to our partners.

The Japanese company experienced a reduction in consumer demand but changes have been made to the product range and the number of retail outlets served has been increased. A new joint venture has been established, with our existing associates, to laminate foam and fabric for the automotive industry using know-how from Vita-tex.

Continued low levels of demand from the automotive industry restricted the company in Indonesia.

In New Zealand the operation had a good year in spite of many difficulties due to market uncertainty, change of government and currency weakness.

Vita Pacific in its first full year as an Australian public company initially suffered a set back in profitability but significant improvement was attained in the second half and continues into the current year. A new foam plant was installed at the major site in Melbourne and other significant investment projects are currently being planned.

7

Directors' Report

The directors have pleasure in presenting their annual report and the accounts for the year ended 31 December 1985.

Profit and dividends

The profit for the year ended 31 December 1985 is £3,717,000 in the Group and £2,492,000 in the Company before provision for dividends of £2,116,000. Retained profit for the year of £1,601,000 has been transferred to reserves.

An interim dividend of 3.3p per Ordinary share was paid on 11 November 1985. The directors now propose a final dividend of 3.7p per Ordinary share payable on 9 May 1986 to shareholders on the Register on 27 March 1986. The total Ordinary dividend for the year is 7p (6.2p) per share.

Principal activities

The Group is principally concerned with the manufacture of cellular foams, synthetic fibre fillings, specialised and coated fabrics, polymeric compounds and mouldings and a range of related consumer products. In addition, recent acquisitions have significantly extended the Group interests in licensing of advanced technical processes.

The Group's principal subsidiary and associated companies are listed on pages 26 and 27. In the UK many of the Group's operations are conducted through manufacturing divisions of British Vita PLC including Vitafoam, Vitaluxan/Portways, Vita Salford, Vitacom, Vitaluxe, Vitamol and Vita Consumer Fibres. The specialised fabric and yarn knitting operations of S. A. Driver, S & T (Barnstaple) and Wildon Knitting are conducted through Vita-tex Limited.

A review of the business and principal operations of the Group is set out on pages 6 and 7, which form part of this report.

Subsidiary companies

In July 1985 the Group purchased for £6.4m in cash the foam interests of the Solvay Group.

Draka Interfoam BV and Veenendaal en Co BV, based in the Netherlands, are involved in the manufacture and supply of polyether foam. These operations are being integrated with the Group's existing Netherlands interests through a new holding company, Vita Interfoam BV.

Unifoam AG in Switzerland controls the worldwide patent licences for the Maxfoam polyether foam manufacturing process.

In Germany, Veenendaal Schaumstoffwerk GmbH and Koepp AG have two production units and six strategically located conversion units supplying the bedding, furniture, automotive, packaging and household product industries with polyether and polyester foams and other speciality products.

There is ongoing uncertainty surrounding the remission of profits from the Zambian subsidiaries due to the continuing shortage of foreign currency in Zambia, which resulted in an auction system for foreign currency with a related major devaluation of the Kwacha being introduced in October 1985. Therefore the Board has concluded that it is no longer appropriate to include the results relating to the Group's Zambian interests in the Consolidated Profit and Loss Account. The 1984 figures have been restated accordingly.

The Group's interest in its two Zambian subsidiaries is shown in the Group Balance Sheet at 31 December 1985 under investments as an amount of £649,000. This reflects retranslating, at the effective exchange rate at 31 December 1985, the value of £4,474,000 in the 1984 Group Balance Sheet. The difference of £3,825,000 has been dealt with through reserves.

Assets in the 1984 Group Balance Sheet totalling £2,110,000 representing blocked funds in Zambia were realised for the sum of £287,000 which has been remitted to the UK. The loss of £1,823,000 is included in extraordinary items.

Directors and other interests

The directors currently holding office are listed on page 2. Mr J. H. Ogden, a non-executive director who does not have a service contract with the Company, retires at the Annual General Meeting and being eligible offers himself for re-election.

Mr N. M. Grimshaw resigned as a director on 23 July 1985. The resignations of Mr W. E. Holt as a director and secretary and of Mr T. Richardson as a director took effect on 31 December 1985.

The interests of the directors in the Ordinary share capital of the Company, including options under employee share option schemes, as at 31 December 1985 are shown on page 9. There has been no change in their interests between 31 December 1985 and 25 February 1986.

8

31 December 1985

	Beneficial	Non-beneficial	Options
F. A. Parker	1,427,337	1,526,096	—
R. McGee	167,534	702,377	39,834
G. Blunt	143,342	—	—
F. J. Eaton	65,215	—	33,988
D. R. Hine	31,775	—	41,000
L. D. Lawton	137,072	—	34,147
J. H. Ogden	21,002	1,832,798	—
R. H. Sellers	35,500	702,377	44,505

Duplications in the table of non-beneficial interest amount to 2,930,850 (3,430,850) Ordinary shares.

In addition, Mr J. H. Ogden has a non-beneficial interest in 1,000 (1,000) Preference shares.

31 December 1984

	Beneficial	Non-beneficial	Options
F. A. Parker	1,427,337	2,026,096	—
R. McGee	167,534	702,377	37,576
G. Blunt	168,342	—	2,576
F. J. Eaton	68,229	—	32,859
D. R. Hine	31,775	—	41,000
L. D. Lawton	142,013	—	33,077
J. H. Ogden	21,002	2,385,298	—
R. H. Sellers	38,005	702,377	43,602

No director has any interest in any of the Company's debentures nor any significant interest in any contract or arrangement entered into by the Company or its subsidiaries.

So far as the directors are aware no person or group of persons, other than certain directors and Legal and General Assurance Society (holding 1,753,687 Ordinary shares representing 5.81%) held an interest comprising 5% or more in the issued share capital of the Company as at 25 February 1986.

Share capital

The Companies Act 1985 requires that any equity shares issued wholly for cash must be offered to existing shareholders in proportion to their existing holdings, although this may be modified by resolution of shareholders. Such a modification is necessary so as to overcome the practical difficulties that might otherwise arise on a rights issue and also to permit issues for cash otherwise than by way of rights to a limited extent. To this end, a special resolution was passed in 1984 expiring on the date of the forthcoming Annual General Meeting. Accordingly Resolution Number 5 will be proposed as a special resolution at the Annual General Meeting to renew this authority to the directors concerning the allotment of equity securities for cash. In the case of allotments other than for rights issues, the authority is limited to shares representing 5% of the authorised capital of the Company. This authority is sought for a further year with the intention of seeking renewal annually.

Fixed assets

Excluding the investment in new subsidiaries, expenditure by the Group on tangible fixed assets during the year was £9,568,000. This included £2.8m to purchase the freehold interest of the factory in Bavaria occupied by one of the newly acquired German companies. Details of the tangible fixed assets are given on page 20.

Close company provisions

The Company is not a close company within the provisions of the Income and Corporation Taxes Act 1970.

Personnel

Through the medium of the Vita magazine and the in-house newspaper, the Group continues to keep its employees informed on its developments throughout the UK and overseas. Apart from the financial extracts included therein, the full report and accounts and the interim statement are made available for all employees.

Well-established consultative committee arrangements are actively maintained, together with collective bargaining procedures with recognised Trade Unions.

Employee involvement in the performance of the Group has been encouraged since the first share option scheme was established in 1974. An approved savings related scheme was created in 1981 and the executive option scheme was established in 1984 (details are provided on page 24 of this report).

The Group gives proper consideration to all applications for employment from disabled persons. Those who are appointed, together with any disabled during employment, receive with their able-bodied colleagues appropriate training for career development and promotion.

Donations

Charitable donations made by the Group during the year amounted to £8,000.

Auditors

A resolution proposing the re-appointment of Arthur Andersen & Co. as auditors of the Company will be put to the Annual General Meeting.

By order of the Board

A. R. Teague

7 March 1986   *Secretary*

9

British Vita Group 1981-1985

£000

	1981*	1982*	1983*	1984*	1984 (restated – note 2)	1985
Turnover and profit						
Company and subsidiaries' turnover	91,869	97,799	109,677	138,391	133,950	186,108
Total associated companies' turnover	89,670	103,377	106,969	127,833	127,833	107,585
Global turnover	181,539	201,176	216,646	266,224	261,783	293,693
Operating profit	5,648	5,063	7,947	9,528	7,824	11,790
Share of profit of associated companies	3,385	3,447	3,520	3,884	3,884	2,584
Interest	(1,062)	(1,126)	(891)	(1,561)	(1,260)	(2,143)
Profit on ordinary activities before taxation:	7,971	7,384	10,576	11,851	10,448	12,231
United Kingdom and Europe	2,428	1,562	5,032	5,943	6,061	9,202
International	5,543	5,822	5,544	5,908	4,387	3,029
Taxation	(3,473)	(3,513)	(3,876)	(4,415)	(3,731)	(5,075)
Minority interests	(91)	(99)	(123)	(134)	(92)	(70)
Extraordinary items and Preference dividend	(598)	(503)	(420)	(941)	(941)	(3,371)
Profit for the year	3,809	3,269	6,157	6,361	5,684	3,715
Ordinary dividend	(1,444)	(1,464)	(1,609)	.(1,868)	(1,868)	(2,114)
Retained profit	2,365	1,805	4,548	4,493	3,816	1,601
Total assets less current liabilities						
Tangible fixed assets	23,547	23,854	24,001	33,425	30,839	41,034
Investments	10,583	12,243	12,963	14,339	18,813	12,389
Net current assets	12,700	12,733	15,141	13,981	11,841	9,947
	46,830	48,830	52,105	61,745	61,493	63,370
Capital employed						
Creditors falling due after more than one year, provisions for liabilities and charges, and minority interests	7,811	7,511	7,283	10,959	10,707	17,299
Capital and reserves	39,019	41,319	44,822	50,786	50,786	46,071
	46,830	48,830	52,105	61,745	61,493	63,370
Ratios						
Operating profit as a percentage of Company and subsidiaries' turnover	6.1%	5.2%	7.3%	6.9%	5.8%	6.3%
Profit on ordinary activities before taxation and interest as a percentage of average capital employed	20%	18%	23%	24%	21%	23%
Earnings per share†	15.0p	12.7p	22.0p	24.3p	22.0p	23.5p
Dividend per share†	4.91p	4.91p	5.36p	6.2p	6.2p	7.0p
Number of times covered	2.6	2.2	3.8	3.4	3.0	1.8
Net assets per share†	133p	138p	149p	169p	169p	153p

†Adjusted for the 1984 capitalisation issue.
*Not reflecting change in basis of accounting for Zambian interests

10

Report of the Auditors

To the Members of British Vita PLC

We have audited the accounts set out on pages 12 to 27 in accordance with approved Auditing Standards.

In our opinion the accounts, which have been prepared under the historical cost convention as modified by the revaluation of certain fixed assets, give a true and fair view of the state of affairs of the Company and the Group at 31 December 1985 and of the profit and source and application of funds of the Group for the year then ended and comply with the Companies Act 1985.

7 March 1986

Arthur Andersen & Co.,
Chartered Accountants,
Manchester

11

Consolidated Profit and Loss Account

for the year ended 31 December 1985

£000

	Notes	1985	1984 (restated – note 2)	1984
Turnover	3	**186,108**	133,950	138,391
Cost of sales		**(144,144)**	(104,137)	(105,987)
Gross profit		**41,964**	29,813	32,404
Distribution costs		**(10,434)**	(7,766)	(8,061)
Administrative expenses		**(19,740)**	(14,223)	(14,815)
Operating profit	4	**11,790**	7,824	9,528
Share of profit of associated companies	5	**2,584**	3,884	3,884
Interest	6	**(2,143)**	(1,260)	(1,561)
Profit on ordinary activities before taxation	3	**12,231**	10,448	11,851
Taxation	7	**(5,075)**	(3,731)	(4,415)
Profit on ordinary activities after taxation		**7,156**	6,717	7,436
Minority interests		**(70)**	(92)	(134)
Profit before extraordinary items		**7,086**	6,625	7,302
Extraordinary items less taxation	8	**(3,369)**	(939)	(939)
Profit for the year		**3,717**	5,686	6,363
Dividends paid and proposed	9	**(2,116)**	(1,870)	(1,870)
Retained profit for the year	24	**1,601**	3,816	4,493

Retained by:			
The Company		376	877
Subsidiary companies		201	3,175
Associated companies		1,024	441
		1,601	4,493

Earnings per share	10	**23.5p**	22.0p	24.3p

Notes on pages 15 to 27 form part of the accounts.

12

Balance Sheets

as at 31 December 1985

£000

	Notes	Group 1985	Group 1984 (restated – note 2)	Company 1985	Company 1984
Fixed assets					
Tangible assets	12	**41,034**	30,839	**8,853**	8,737
Investments	13	**12,389**	18,813	**11,482**	11,652
		53,423	49,652	**20,335**	20,389
Current assets					
Stocks	14	**22,241**	19,530	**7,644**	7,443
Debtors	15	**46,716**	38,872	**23,252**	21,000
Cash at bank and in hand	16	**5,844**	3,394	**4,435**	1,628
		74,801	61,796	**35,331**	30,071
Creditors: amounts falling due within one year	17	**(64,854)**	(49,955)	**(23,786)**	(21,585)
Net current assets		**9,947**	11,841	**11,545**	8,486
Total assets less current liabilities		**63,370**	61,493	**31,880**	28,875
Creditors: amounts falling due after more than one year	17	**15,256**	9,856	**8,818**	6,199
Provisions for liabilities and charges	19	**1,477**	602	**130**	206
Minority interests		**566**	249	**—**	—
Capital and reserves					
Called up share capital	20	**7,607**	7,589	**7,607**	7,589
Share premium account	21	**4,607**	4,537	**4,607**	4,537
Revaluation reserve	22	**3,532**	5,147	**—**	—
Other reserves	23	**7,197**	10,343	**283**	285
Profit and loss account	24	**23,128**	23,170	**10,435**	10,059
		46,071	50,786	**22,932**	22,470
Capital employed		**63,370**	61,493	**31,880**	28,875

The accounts on pages 12 to 27 were approved by the Board on 7 March 1986 and were signed on its behalf by:

F. A. Parker
R. McGee   Directors

Notes on pages 15 to 27 form part of the accounts.

13

Group Source and Application of Funds

for the year ended 31 December 1985

£000

	1985	1984 (restated – note 2)
Source of funds		
Profit on ordinary activities before tax less minority interests	12,161	10,356
Extraordinary items	(3,369)	(939)
	8,792	9,417
Items not involving the movement of funds		
Minority interest in the profit retained for the year	70	92
Depreciation	4,850	3,511
Profit retained by associated companies	(1,024)	(441)
Exchange differences and other items	80	(614)
Total funds generated from operations	12,768	11,965
Funds from other sources		
Sale of tangible fixed assets	534	645
Issue of Ordinary share capital	86	104
Increase in creditors: amounts falling due after more than one year	—	940
Decrease in investment in associated companies	324	—
Decrease in debtors: amounts falling due after more than one year	382	—
Increase in loans	5,361	256
	19,455	13,910
Application of funds		
Dividends paid	1,962	1,725
Taxation paid	3,193	2,580
Acquisition of subsidiaries*	5,786	2,150
Decrease in creditors: amounts falling due after more than one year	819	—
Increase in investment in associated companies	—	385
Increase in debtors: amounts falling due after more than one year	—	1,158
Purchase of tangible fixed assets	9,568	8,248
Working capital movement		
Increase (decrease) in stocks	(416)	4,009
Increase (decrease) in debtors: amounts falling due within one year	(1,138)	2,983
Increase in creditors: amounts falling due within one year	(6,566)	(3,733)
	13,208	19,505
Increase (decrease) in net cash balances	6,247	(5,595)

*Analysis of subsidiaries acquired

Net assets acquired	
Tangible fixed assets	6,353
Current assets	13,830
Creditors	
Amounts falling due within one year	(11,733)
Amounts falling due after more than one year	(564)
Provisions for liabilities and charges	(894)
Minority interests	(345)
Net tangible assets	6,647
Goodwill on acquisition	(861)
Discharged by cash	5,786

14

Accounting Policies

1 Basis of accounts The accounts are prepared under the historical cost convention modified to include the revaluation of certain fixed assets.

2 Basis of consolidation The consolidated accounts include the accounts of the Company and its subsidiaries and the Group's share of the results and post-acquisition reserves of associated companies.

The results relating to the Group's interests in Zambia have been excluded in 1985 and restated comparative figures are given in the Consolidated Profit and Loss Account and Group Balance Sheet (see note 2).

The Company accounts and those of its UK and European subsidiaries are made up to 31 December and, for administrative reasons, the accounts of the international subsidiaries are made up to 30 September.

The results of the associated companies adjusted as appropriate to accord with the Group's accounting policies are included on the basis of audited accounts for a period ending not more than six months before 31 December. Associated companies are also related companies as defined in the Companies Act 1985. There are no other related companies.

The assets of companies acquired during the year are incorporated at their fair value at the date of acquisition. The goodwill arising on the acquisition of subsidiaries is dealt with through distributable reserves.

3 Foreign currency balances are translated at the rate of exchange at the year end. Exchange differences arising from the translation of the opening balance sheets of subsidiary and associated companies, net of differences on related currency borrowings, are dealt with through reserves. Other gains and losses are dealt with in the Profit and Loss Account.

4 Turnover represents the net amounts invoiced to external customers but excludes value added and sales taxes and any part of the sales of associated companies.

5 Depreciation of tangible fixed assets is provided at rates estimated to write off the cost or valuation of assets over their useful lives, the principal rates of annual straight line depreciation being:

(a) Freehold buildings 2½%.

(b) Leasehold land and buildings 2½% or over the period of the lease if less than forty years.

(c) Plant between 10% and 33⅓%.

(d) Vehicles between 16% and 25%.

6 Stocks are valued at the lower of first-in, first-out cost and net realisable value; cost includes appropriate production overhead expenses.

7 Grants on assets are credited to the Profit and Loss Account over the lives of the relevant assets. Other grants are credited to revenue in the year in which the expenditure to which they relate is charged.

8 Research and development, patents and trade marks expenditure is charged against profit of the year in which it is incurred.

9 Pensions The Group funds pension liabilities, on the advice of independent actuaries, by contributing to independent trusts or to insurance companies. The cost of these contributions is charged against the profit of the year.

10 Taxation UK and overseas taxation is provided on taxable profits at appropriate local current rates. Provision is made for deferred taxation in circumstances where there is a reasonable probability of payment in the foreseeable future. The provision is established at corporation tax rates anticipated to be in force at the time the deferred liability is expected to crystallise. Advance corporation tax which is available to reduce the corporation tax payable on future profits is carried forward and, to the extent appropriate, is deducted from the provision for deferred taxation.

15

Notes to the Accounts

£000

---

1 Company profit and loss account

In accordance with Section 228(7) of the Companies Act 1985 the Company has not presented a separate profit and loss account.

2 Change in basis of accounting for Zambian interests

There is ongoing uncertainty surrounding the remission of profits from the Zambian subsidiaries due to the continuing shortage of foreign currency in Zambia, which resulted in an auction system for foreign currency with a related major devaluation of the Kwacha being introduced in October 1985. Therefore the Board has concluded that it is no longer appropriate to include the results relating to the Group's Zambian interests in the Consolidated Profit and Loss Account. The 1984 restated figures exclude turnover of £4,441,000 and profit on ordinary activities before taxation of £1,403,000.

The figures for the Zambian subsidiaries excluded from the 1985 Consolidated Profit and Loss Account are turnover of £900,000 and profit on ordinary activities before taxation of £291,000, translated at the effective exchange rate at 31 December 1985.

The Group's interest in its two Zambian subsidiaries is shown in the Group Balance Sheet at 31 December 1985 under investments as an amount of £649,000. This reflects retranslating, at the effective exchange rate at 31 December 1985, the value of £4,474,000 in the 1984 Group Balance Sheet. The difference of £3,825,000 has been dealt with through reserves.

The restated 1984 Group Balance Sheet reflects the following changes to reclassify the assets and liabilities of the Zambian subsidiaries under one heading within investments:

Reduction in:		
Tangible fixed assets	2,586	
Stocks	2,542	
Debtors	736	
Cash at bank and in hand	1,030	
		6,894
Creditors — amounts falling due within one year	2,168	
Minority interests	252	
		(2,420)
Reclassified in investments		4,474

Group capital and reserves at 31 December 1984 are not affected by the above reclassification.

Assets in the 1984 Group Balance Sheet totalling £2,110,000, representing blocked funds in Zambia, were realised for the sum of £287,000 which has been remitted to the UK. The loss of £1,823,000 is included in extraordinary items.

All 1984 Group comparative figures in Notes to the Accounts on pages 17 to 23 are shown on the restated basis.

16

3 Analysis of turnover and profit

Turnover (excluding associated companies) and profit on ordinary activities before taxation (including share of profit of associated companies) attributable to major business groupings:

	1985		1984 (restated)	
	Turnover	Profit	Turnover	Profit
UK	109,629	4,476	97,341	4,548
Europe	74,976	4,726	34,484	1,513
International	1,503	3,029	2,125	4,387
	186,108	12,231	133,950	10,448

Turnover by geographical market:

	1985	1984
UK	100,833	89,613
Europe: Benelux	16,399	10,466
France	39,866	19,466
Germany	17,521	4,343
Other	4,392	4,155
	78,178	38,430
Africa	3,523	3,062
Rest of world	3,574	2,845
	186,108	133,950

	1985	1984 (restated)
4 Operating profit		
After charging:		
Depreciation	4,850	3,509
Leasing of plant and vehicles	719	407
Auditors' remuneration	240	164
After crediting:		
Government grants	120	116
5 Share of profit of associated companies		
Total turnover	107,585	127,833
Share of profit less losses	2,584	3,884
Taxation	(1,037)	(1,577)
Extraordinary items less taxation	108	(21)
	1,655	2,286
Less receivable as dividends	(631)	(1,845)
Retained by associated companies	1,024	441
6 Interest		
Bank overdrafts, acceptance credits and bank loans	2,285	1,278
Loans not fully repayable within five years	123	144
Loan notes	1	15
	2,409	1,437
Less interest received	(266)	(177)
	2,143	1,260

17

Notes to the Accounts

(continued)

£000

	1985	1984 (restated)
7 Taxation		
UK:		
Corporation tax on the profit for the year at 41.25% (46.25%)	2,713	1,684
Deferred taxation (credit) charge for the year at 35%	(30)	600
Double tax relief	(577)	(742)
	2,106	1,542
Overseas tax	1,932	612
Associated companies – tax on share of profit	1,037	1,577
	5,075	3,731

The UK tax charge for the year has been increased (reduced) by the following:

Stock relief	—	(106)
Capital allowances shortfall (excess) against depreciation	341	(894)
Tax losses brought forward	—	(58)
	341	(1,058)

There are advance corporation tax credits carried forward of £2,063,000 (£2,310,000) in the Group and in the Company.

Provision for deferred taxation (note 19) has been made in respect of:

	Group		Company	
	1985	1984 (restated)	1985	1984
Excess of capital allowances over depreciation				
of tangible fixed assets	1,927	1,763	913	1,443
Advance corporation tax recoverable	(1,430)	(1,411)	(783)	(1,237)
	497	352	130	206

If full provision had been made, the total would have been:*

Excess of capital allowances over depreciation				
of tangible fixed assets	4,569	4,509	2,545	2,695
Advance corporation tax recoverable	(1,430)	(1,411)	(783)	(1,237)
	3,139	3,098	1,762	1,458

*These amounts do not include any provision for tax on capital gains which might arise on disposal at book values of properties which are held for long term use in the Group's business.

	1985	1984 (restated)
8 Extraordinary items less taxation		
Loss (profit) on disposal of associated companies	(62)	98
Closure and restructuring costs	2,178	1,704
Loss on realisation of assets blocked in Zambia	1,823	—
	3,939	1,802
Less taxation	(570)	(455)
	3,369	1,347
Provision at 35% for deferred taxation		
net of advance corporation tax	—	(408)
	3,369	939

18

£000

	1985	1984 (restated)
9 Dividends		
Ordinary shares:		
Interim – paid	**996**	904
Final – proposed	**1,118**	964
Total Ordinary dividends paid and proposed	**2,114**	1,868
4.2% Cumulative Preference shares	**2**	2
	2,116	1,870

10 Earnings per share

The calculation of net earnings per Ordinary share of 25p is based on earnings (after minority interests and Preference dividend but before extraordinary items) of £7,084,000 (£6,623,000 as restated) and on 30,138,283 (30,062,940) shares, being the weighted average of Ordinary shares in issue during the year.

11 Employees and directors

Employment costs:

	1985	1984
Wages and salaries	**32,706**	24,091
Social security costs	**5,397**	3,668
Other pension costs	**2,028**	1,255
	40,131	29,014

Average numbers employed:

	1985	1984 (restated)
UK	**2,670**	2,589
Europe	**1,263**	668
International	**73**	105
Company and subsidiaries	**4,006**	3,362
Associated companies	**3,549**	3,724
	7,555	7,086

Directors' emoluments including pension contributions:

	1985	1984
as directors	**30**	17
as executives	**533**	575
Pension and pension contributions to former directors	**9**	9
Payments including pension contributions to past directors on cessation of executive employment	**227**	—
	799	601

Directors' emoluments, excluding pension contributions, include:

	1985	1984
Chairman	**20**	33
Highest paid director	**67**	51

Other directors

	1985	1984		1985	1984
Below £5,000	–	1			
£5,001–£10,000	1	1			
£10,001–£15,000	1	–	UK senior employees		
£30,001–£35,000	1	–		4	1
£35,001–£40,000	1	2		2	–
£40,001–£45,000	3	2		–	1
£45,001–£50,000	–	4		–	–
£50,001–£55,000	2	–		–	–

19

Notes to the Accounts

(continued)

£000

12 Tangible fixed assets	Group				Company
	Land	Buildings	Plant & vehicles	Total	Plant & vehicles
Cost and valuation					
Balance 31 December 1984*	3,313	10,661	34,437	48,411	18,058
Exchange rate adjustment	29	46	74	149	—
Additions	297	4,528	4,743	9,568	2,153
New subsidiaries	781	5,534	8,615	14,930	—
Disposals	(25)	(25)	(1,521)	(1,571)	(615)
Revaluation adjustment	—	(424)	—	(424)	—
Balance 31 December 1985†	4,395	20,320	46,348	71,063	19,596
Accumulated depreciation					
Balance 31 December 1984*	—	—	17,572	17,572	9,321
Exchange rate adjustment	—	—	(60)	(60)	—
New subsidiaries	—	2,936	5,641	8,577	—
Disposals	—	—	(1,159)	(1,159)	(443)
Charge for year	—	739	4,111	4,850	1,865
Charge in extraordinary items	—	—	249	249	—
Balance 31 December 1985	—	3,675	26,354	30,029	10,743
Net book value					
31 December 1985	4,395	16,645	19,994	41,034	8,853
31 December 1984*	3,313	10,661	16,865	30,839	8,737
†Cost and valuation analysis:					
Valuation: 1984*	3,317	10,258	—	13,575	—
Cost	1,078	10,062	46,348	57,488	19,596
	4,395	20,320	46,348	71,063	19,596

Land and buildings comprise:

Freehold	23,163
Long leasehold	1,040
Short leasehold	512
	24,715

If land ,and buildings had not been revalued they would have been included at Cost of £25,549,000 (£13,157,000*) less Accumulated depreciation of £8,579,000 (£4,813,000*).

Capital commitments
Commitments for capital expenditure at 31 December 1985 not provided for in the accounts amounted to £667,000 (£867,000) for the Group and £50,000 (£52,000) for the Company. In addition capital expenditure authorised by the directors but not contracted amounted to £315,000 (£750,000) for the Group and £100,000 (£297,000) for the Company.
The Group also has commitments in respect of plant and vehicle finance leasing agreements totalling £87,000 (£74,000) of which £23,000 (£33,000) arises in 1986.

*As restated

20

£000

13 Investments	Group				Company		
	Subsidiary companies	Associated companies Listed	Unlisted	Total	Subsidiary companies	Associated company	Total
Shares at cost less amounts written off							
Balance 31 December 1984	—	23	1,477	1,500	6,537	175	6,712
Exchange rate adjustments and miscellaneous	—	(1)	(8)	(9)	—	—	—
Additions at cost	—	—	24	24	—	—	—
Disposals	—	—	(45)	(45)	—	—	—
	—	22	1,448	1,470	6,537	175	6,712
Share of post acquisition reserves							
Balance 31 December 1984	—	7,488	4,358	11,846	—	—	—
Exchange rate adjustments and miscellaneous	—	(1,998)	(1,099)	(3,097)	—	—	—
Disposals	—	—	(249)	(249)	—	—	—
Share of retained profit	—	329	695	1,024	—	—	—
Shares at cost and share of post acquisition reserves 31 December 1985††	—	5,841	5,153	10,994	6,537	175	6,712
Investment in subsidiaries							
Balance 31 December 1984	4,474	—	—	4,474	—	—	—
Exchange rate adjustments and miscellaneous	(3,825)	—	—	(3,825)	—	—	—
Balance 31 December 1985	649	—	—	649	—	—	—
Loans							
Balance 31 December 1984	—	—	993	993	4,800	140	4,940
Exchange rate adjustments	—	—	(193)	(193)	—	—	—
Repayments	—	—	(54)	(54)	—	(20)	(20)
Written off	—	—	—	—	(150)	—	(150)
Balance 31 December 1985	—	—	746	746	4,650	120	4,770
Net book value							
31 December 1985	649	5,841	5,899†	12,389	11,187	295	11,482
31 December 1984	4,474	7,511	6,828†	18,813*	11,337	315	11,652

††Market value of shares listed overseas and directors' valuation of unlisted shares in associated companies

		Listed	Unlisted	Total		Associated	Total
31 December 1985		4,428	7,500	11,928		600	600
31 December 1984		6,238	8,600	14,838		600	600

†Net book value includes goodwill of £538,000 (£65,000).
*As restated.

21

Notes to the Accounts

(continued)

£000

	Group		Company	
	1985	1984 (restated)	1985	1984
14 Stocks				
Raw materials and consumable stores	14,242	13,877	5,672	5,956
Work in progress and finished goods	7,999	5,653	1,972	1,487
	22,241	19,530	7,644	7,443
15 Debtors				
Amounts falling due within one year				
Trade debtors	40,728	33,029	15,788	14,336
Amounts owed by subsidiary companies	—	—	4,511	3,883
Amounts owed by associated companies	617	781	185	358
Other debtors	2,387	1,567	664	834
Prepayments and accrued income	1,375	1,238	727	626
	45,107	36,615	21,875	20,037
Amounts falling due after more than one year				
Amounts owed by associated companies	612	1,049	—	—
Other debtors	364	309	97	64
Advance corporation tax	633	899	1,280	899
	46,716	38,872	23,252	21,000
16 Cash at bank and in hand				
Cash at Zambian banks awaiting remittance approval	—	1,718	—	13
Cash at bank and in hand	5,844	1,676	4,435	1,615
	5,844	3,394	4,435	1,628
17 Creditors				
Amounts falling due within one year				
Bank overdrafts—secured by fixed charges	1,862	1,169	—	—
Bank overdrafts—unsecured	8,139	10,506	1,500	1,019
Current portion of loans (note 18)	975	866	—	9
Other loans	76	213	76	213
	11,052	12,754	1,576	1,241
Trade creditors	35,857	27,779	16,853	15,212
Bills payable	147	306	79	—
Amounts owed to subsidiary companies	—	—	—	983
Amounts owed to associated companies	—	64	—	61
Corporation tax	2,857	2,086	626	937
Other taxes and social security costs	4,073	2,537	1,701	867
Other creditors	5,031	1,465	408	382
Accruals and deferred income	4,719	2,000	1,425	938
Proposed dividend	1,118	964	1,118	964
	64,854	49,955	23,786	21,585
Amounts falling due after more than one year				
Loans (note 18)	14,270	8,454	7,266	4,630
Amounts due to subsidiary companies	—	—	1,360	1,361
Corporation tax	275	—	—	—
Deferred income—government grants	600	472	174	190
Other creditors	111	930	18	18
	15,256	9,856	8,818	6,199

22

£000

		Group		Company	
18 Loans		**1985**	1984 (restated)	**1985**	1984
Long term (not wholly repayable within 5 years)					
UK:	7¼% debenture stock 1987/92	**293**	309	**293**	309
	10¼% debenture stock 1990/95	**652**	762	**652**	762
	Bank loan 1988/92	**3,500**	3,500	**3,500**	3,500
	Bf bank loan 1986/89	**—**	827	**—**	—
Overseas:	FFr bank loans 1986/95	**1,993**	2,236	**—**	—
Medium term (repayable within 5 years)					
UK:	Loan notes 1986	**—**	68	**—**	68
	Dm bank loan 1989	**2,821**	—	**2,821**	—
	Bf bank loan 1986/90	**664**	—	**—**	—
Overseas:	Bf bank loans 1986/89	**612**	1,013	**—**	—
	Dfl bank loan 1986	**3,254**	486	**—**	—
	Dm bank loan 1986/89	**1,407**	—	**—**	—
	FFr bank loans 1986/88	**49**	119	**—**	—
		15,245	9,320	**7,266**	4,639

Interest charges on the bank loans are linked to inter-bank rates relative to the currency borrowed except for £1,040,000 of the Dm bank loans at fixed rates, averaging 6.9%. All overseas loans are secured by fixed charges except for £1,790,000 of the FFr loan and £246,000 of the Dm loans. The debenture stocks are secured by floating charge. The UK bank loans are unsecured. The loans are repayable as follows:

between one and two years	**1,909**	1,173	**—**	9
between two and five years	**9,410**	3,140	**4,921**	1,450
over five years	**2,951**	4,141	**2,345**	3,171
Amounts falling due after more than one year (note 17)	**14,270**	8,454	**7,266**	4,630
Amounts falling due within one year (note 17)	**975**	866	**—**	9
	15,245	9,320	**7,266**	4,639

19 Provisions for liabilities and charges

Deferred taxation (note 7)	**497**	352	**130**	206
Pensions provision	**980**	250	**—**	—
	1,477	602	**130**	206

Movements:	Total	Deferred taxation	Pensions
Balance 31 December 1984	602	352	250
Exchange rate adjustment	10	3	7
Current year charge	111	142	(31)
New subsidiaries	754	—	754
Balance 31 December 1985	1,477	497	980

23

Notes to the Accounts

(continued)

£000

	1985	1984	1985	1984
20 Share capital			Allotted, called up and fully paid	
		Authorised		
4.2% Cumulative Preference shares of £1 each (60,000 authorised, 57,450 allotted)	**60**	60	**57**	57
Ordinary shares of 25p each (38,000,000 authorised, 30,200,302 allotted)	**9,500**	9,500	**7,550**	7,532
	9,560	9,560	**7,607**	7,589

In 1985, 72,275 Ordinary shares were allotted, fully paid, under the employee share schemes.

Employee share options

Employee participation in the Company has been encouraged by share option schemes since 1975 when the first options of the schemes approved in 1974 were offered. The Own As You Earn Scheme was concluded in 1985 upon the maturing of the final options granted under that Scheme in 1980. Options under the 1974 Executive and International schemes, exercisable between the third and seventh anniversaries of the grant, are still outstanding at 31 December 1985 involving 148,670 shares at prices between 140p and 162p.

In 1981 the British Vita Savings Related Share Option Scheme was adopted, replacing the Own As You Earn Scheme. Options under this Scheme are exercisable on the fifth anniversary of the grant and there are 516,087 share options outstanding at 31 December 1985 at prices between 110p and 176.4p. These include options over 166,003 shares granted in 1985 at a subscription price of 163.8p.

In November 1984, the first options were granted under the British Vita Executive Share Option Scheme 1984 and Vita International Share Option Scheme 1984. No options were granted in 1985 and options outstanding at 31 December 1985 are 880,000 shares at 165p, normally exercisable between the third and tenth anniversaries of the grant.

As at 31 December 1985, there are a further 1,615.943 shares available for future grants of options under the present schemes.

	Group		Company	
21 Share premium account				
Balance 31 December 1984	**4,537**	5,138	**4,537**	5,138
Bonus capitalisation	**—**	(682)	**—**	(682)
Premium on shares issued	**70**	81	**70**	81
Balance 31 December 1985	**4,607**	4,537	**4,607**	4,537
22 Revaluation reserve				
Balance 31 December 1984	**5,147**	4,111	**—**	—
Exchange rate adjustments and miscellaneous	**(1,133)**	(60)	**—**	—
Property revaluation	**—**	778	**—**	—
Property revaluation adjustment	**(424)**	—	**—**	—
Transfer from profit and loss account (note 24):				
Adjustment on revaluation	**(57)**	565	**—**	—
Transfer to other reserves (note 23)	**(1)**	(247)	**—**	—
Balance 31 December 1985 (including reserves of associated companies of £409,000 (£526,000))	**3,532**	5,147	**—**	—
23 Other reserves				
Balance 31 December 1984	**10,343**	8,902	**285**	121
Exchange rate adjustments and miscellaneous	**(4,497)**	(168)	**—**	172
Share option capitalisation	**(2)**	(8)	**(2)**	(8)
Transfer from profit and loss account (note 24)	**1,352**	1,370	**—**	—
Transfer from revaluation reserve (note 22)	**1**	247	**—**	—
Balance 31 December 1985 (including reserves of associated companies of £4,195,000 (£6,097,000))	**7,197**	10,343	**283**	285

24

£000

	Group		Company	
	1985	1984	**1985**	1984
24 Profit and loss account				
Balance 31 December 1984	**23,170**	19,795	**10,059**	9,367
Exchange rate adjustments and miscellaneous	**(1,209)**	493	**—**	11
Transfer from revaluation reserve (note 22):				
Adjustment on revaluation	**57**	(565)	**—**	—
Retained profit for the year	**1,601**	4,493	**376**	877
Goodwill on acquisition	**861**	324	**—**	(196)
Transfer to other reserves (note 23)	**(1,352)**	(1,370)	**—**	—
Balance 31 December 1985 (including retained profit of associated companies of £4,920,000 (£5,222,000))	**23,128**	23,170	**10,435**	10,059

Of total reserves shown in the Balance Sheets, the profit and loss account reserves are regarded as distributable.

The dividends received in the UK and Europe during the year from international operations were £766,000 (£1,005,000). The Group operates in several overseas countries where dividends are restricted by local legislation and at 31 December 1985 retained profits of £136,000 (£605,000) for subsidiaries and of £1,492,000 (£1,682,000) for associated companies were so restricted. In addition there are exchange control restrictions in certain overseas countries on the remittance of funds abroad. If the retained reserves on overseas companies were distributed as dividends they would be liable to overseas taxes and, subject to double tax relief, UK taxation. As no such distributions are likely in the foreseeable future, no provision has been made.

25 Pensions

In the UK contributions at rates recommended by independent Actuaries and reviewed biennially are made to contributory schemes constituted as separate trust funds. The Actuaries have advised that as at 5 April 1985, the date of the last biennial actuarial valuation, on the basis of the recommended contribution rates, the schemes were fully funded on both a discontinuance and a going concern basis. Ex gratia pensions are paid to former employees not in receipt of funded pensions at a present cost of £22,000 per annum.

Pension schemes are operated for most European and International companies, to provide benefits to supplement those of state schemes. Where schemes are not operated through insured funds, provision for pension liabilities has been made in these accounts. Employer contributions are liable to adjustment against changing actuarial conditions.

One European subsidiary has a continuing contractual responsibility to pay unfunded pension liabilities to former employees of the group of which it was a member; provision for that liability, as actuarially quantified, has been made in these accounts.

26 Contingent liabilities

The Company has guaranteed certain of the overdrafts and third party liabilities of certain subsidiary companies, amounting to £6,631,000 (£6,196,000).

In addition to pension liabilities referred to in note 25, there were contingent liabilities in connection with legal claims the ascertainable amount of which was £300,000 (£347,000) for the Group and £273,000 (£267,000) for the Company.

The Company has guaranteed borrowings under bank facilities amounting to £54,000 (£81,000) for certain associated companies.

25

Principal Subsidiary Companies

United Kingdom	Country of incorporation and principal operation	Product or activities
Bailey & Williamson Limited	England	Pine beds
British Vita Investments Limited	England	Property management
Caligen Foam Limited	England	Cellular foam products
Chemibond Limited	England	Merchanting
Foam Components Limited	England	Cellular foam products
Vita International Limited	England	Holding company
Vita-tex Limited	England	Specialised fabrics

Europe		
Caligen Europe BV	Netherlands	Cellular foam products
Deutsche Vita Polymere GmbH	Germany	Holding company
Draka Interfoam BV	Netherlands	Cellular foam products
Koepp AG (94.25%)	Germany	Cellular foam products
Libeltex NV	Belgium	Fibre processing
Morard Europe SA	France	Cellular foam products
Tramico SA	France	Cellular foam and polymeric products
Unifoam AG	Switzerland	Patent licensing
Veenendaal en Co BV	Netherlands	Cellular foam products
Veenendaal Schaumstoffwerk GmbH	Germany	Cellular foam products
Vitafoam Europe BV	Netherlands	Holding company
Vita Interfoam BV	Netherlands	Holding company
Vita Polymers Europe BV	Netherlands	Holding company
Vita Polymeres France SA	France	Holding company

International		
Furniture Corporation of Zambia Limited (90%)*	Zambia	Furniture, mattresses and retailing
Vitafoam Kenya Limited (75%)	Kenya	Cellular foam products
Vitafoam Zambia Limited (90%)*	Zambia	Cellular foam products

Notes
1. Unless otherwise indicated 100% of issued share capital is owned by British Vita PLC. Interests in the European and International companies are held through subsidiaries of British Vita PLC.

2. The accounts of all subsidiary companies in the UK and Europe are audited by Arthur Andersen & Co., whilst those of other subsidiaries are audited by other firms.

* The results of these companies are excluded from the Consolidated Profit and Loss Account — see note 2 on page 16.

26

Principal Associated Companies

Name and country of incorporation and principal operation	Equity Total 000's	Company Interest %	Results up to
United Kingdom			
BTR-Vitaline Limited England	£350	50.0	31 Dec
Europe			
Vita Cortex Holdings Limited Ireland	I£529	50.0	31 Dec
International			
Vita Pacific Limited Australia	A$3,000	40.0	30 Jun
Vitafoam Barbados Limited Barbados	B$75	50.0	30 Sep
Vitafoam Products Canada Limited Canada	C$20	50.0	30 Sep
Taki-Vita SAE Egypt	E£2,000	40.0	31 Dec
PT Vitafoam Indonesia Indonesia	Rp273,900	33.5	30 Sep
Vita Colourfoam Japan Limited Japan	Y63,000	20.0	30 Jun
Vitafoam Nigeria Limited Nigeria	N18,200	20.0	30 Sep
Vitafoam SA (Pty) Limited South Africa	R150	50.0	30 Sep
Vitafoam CA (Private) Limited Zimbabwe	Z$1,804	50.0	31 Dec

Notes:
1. BTR-Vitaline Limited is held directly by British Vita PLC and all other associated companies are held through subsidiaries of British Vita PLC.

2. The principal activity of the associated companies is the manufacture of cellular foam products except for BTR-Vitaline Limited which is engaged in plant lining and glass reinforced products.

3. Vita Pacific Limited, which is listed on the Australian Associated Stock Exchanges, holds 25% of Vita Colourfoam Japan Limited and 24.9% of Vita New Zealand Limited. These holdings are excluded from the Company Interest % in the table above.

4. Vita International Limited also holds, indirectly, 50% of the I£10,572 preference shares of Vita Cortex Holdings Limited and 50% of the C$180,000 preference shares of Vitafoam Products Canada Limited.

5. Vitafoam Nigeria Limited is listed on the Nigerian Stock Exchange.

6. The accounts of all associated companies are audited by firms other than Arthur Andersen & Co.

Oyez Press Limited – Birmingham & London

Appendix D: Report of British Vita PLC for the Six Months Ended 30 June 1986

Chairman's Statement

Results

The Group has continued to make good progress across a broad front of its businesses during the first half of 1986 following a good second half in 1985. Turnover grew to £111m representing a 37% increase on the £81m achieved in the first half of 1985. Profit before tax increased to more than £8m, almost £3m higher than the comparative figure for the first half of last year, and earnings per share have increased by over 50% in the same period.

The results in the UK show a steady improvement while the greatly increased European profit is proving the ability of the Group, following upon acquisitions, to generate management cooperation and enthusiasm in differing national and commercial environments.

In my annual review I said that the theme for 1986 was cash generation. I can now report that, as a result of satisfactory cash flow in the first half of the year, Group gearing is down from 42% to 34%.

Dividend

The board has declared an interim dividend of 4p per Ordinary share payable on 10 November 1986 to shareholders on the register at the close of business on 3 October 1986. This represents a 21% increase over the interim dividend of 3.3p paid last year.

The Board is also recommending a capitalisation issue of 1 share for every 2 shares held, details of which are included with this report. The new Ordinary shares will not rank for the interim dividend.

Outlook

The Board is confident that the Group will continue its progress in the second half. There will be continuing emphasis on cash and asset management which, together with the application of modern quality techniques such as statistical process control to manufacturing operations, gives confidence for ongoing growth.

F. A. Carter

8 September 1986   Chairman

2

Group Interim Results

(unaudited) for the six months ended 30 June 1986

Year 1985	£000	First Half 1986	1985
186,108	**Turnover to external customers**	**110,933**	80,867
11,790	**Operating profit**	**7,629**	4,826
2,584	**Share of profit of associated companies**	**1,408**	1,432
(2,143)	**Interest**	**(910)**	(1,010)
12,231	**Profit on ordinary activities before taxation**	**8,127**	5,248
4,476	United Kingdom	**2,505**	2,126
4,726	Europe	**4,159**	1,532
3,029	International	**1,463**	1,590
(5,075)	**Taxation**	**(3,415)**	(2,150)
7,156	**Profit on ordinary activities after taxation**	**4,712**	3,098
(70)	**Minority interests**	**(31)**	(30)
(3,369)	**Extraordinary items less taxation**	**71**	(319)
3,717	**Profit for the period**	**4,752**	2,749
23.5p	**Earnings per share**	**15.5p**	10.2p
7.0p	**Dividend per share**	**4.0p**	3.3p
2,116	**Cost of dividends (£000)**	**1,214**	997

Note:

The accounts in respect of the financial year ended 31 December 1985 are an abridged version of the Company's full accounts, which have been reported on without qualification by the auditors and have been delivered to the Registrar of Companies.

3

BRITISH VITA PLC

(Registered in England No. 871669)

Directors:
F.A. Parker (Chairman)
R. McGee (Chief Executive)
G. Blunt
F.J. Eaton
Secretary: A.R. Teague

D.R. Hine
L.D. Lawton
J.H. Ogden
R.H. Sellers

Registered Office
Soudan Street
Middleton
Manchester
M24 2DB

To the Ordinary Shareholders of the Company and, for information only, to the holders of Cumulative Preference Shares, Debenture Stocks, Guaranteed Unsecured Loan Notes and Share Options.

Dear Shareholder,

Proposed Increase in Authorised Share Capital and Capitalisation Issue

In order to broaden the capital base of the Company it was announced today that your directors have decided to recommend a capitalisation issue on the basis of 1 new Ordinary share for every 2 existing Ordinary shares held at the close of business on 26 September 1986. I am now writing to give you details of the proposed capitalisation issue, the necessary increase in the Company's authorised share capital and certain consequential matters including adjustments to employee share option rights.

Capitalisation Issue

Your directors are recommending a capitalisation issue on a one for two basis to be effected by the issue of 15,160,917 fully paid Ordinary shares of 25p each and by the capitalisation of the sum of £3,790,229.25 being part of the amount now standing to the credit of the Company's share premium account. The new Ordinary shares will not rank for the interim dividend announced today but will otherwise rank *pari passu* in all respects with the existing issued Ordinary shares.

Application will be made to The Stock Exchange for the new Ordinary shares to be admitted to the Official List. It is expected that such listing will become effective on Monday 13 October 1986. Subject to the passing of the appropriate resolutions, including Resolution 2 which authorises the proposed capitalisation issue, the 15,160,917 new Ordinary shares will be allotted credited as fully paid up to shareholders on the register at the close of business on 26 September 1986. Fractional entitlements will not be allotted but will be aggregated and sold for the benefit of the Company.

Renounceable certificates will be posted on 10 October 1986 and dealings are expected to commence on 13 October 1986. The last date for splitting will be 19 November 1986 and the last date for registration of renunciations will be 21 November 1986. After 21 November 1986 the new Ordinary shares will be in registered form and will be transferable only in accordance with the Company's Articles of Association. Pending the posting by 19 December 1986 of definitive certificates in respect of registration after renunciation, transfers will be certified against the register.

Increase in Authorised Share Capital

The number of Ordinary shares at present remaining unissued is not sufficient to permit the proposed capitalisation issue. It is accordingly necessary to increase the authorised share capital of the Company. Your directors also consider that a margin of authorised but unissued Ordinary share capital should be maintained. Resolution 1 of the attached Notice of Meeting therefore provides for the authorised share capital to be increased from £9,560,000 to £16,560,000 by the creation of an additional 28,000,000 Ordinary shares of 25p each.

After this increase and the capitalisation issue there will be 20,517,248 unissued Ordinary shares representing 31.09% of the enlarged authorised Ordinary share capital. However, options under the Company's employee share option schemes are outstanding or available for allocation on 4,568,550 Ordinary shares, leaving 15,948,698 unissued Ordinary shares representing 24.16% of the enlarged authorised Ordinary share capital.

4

Your directors have no present intention of issuing any further shares and no issue will be made which would effectively alter the control of the Company without the prior approval of shareholders in General Meeting.

Employee Share Option Schemes
Outstanding options under the Company's employee share option schemes and the limits to the number of shares available for issue under the schemes will be adjusted proportionately to the capitalisation issue in accordance with the Rules of the Schemes, the manner of such adjustments having been confirmed as fair and reasonable by the Company's auditors as required under those Rules.

Authorities under the Companies Act 1985
The authority of your directors to allot shares is subject to the provisions of Section 80 of the Companies Act 1985. The authority under this section which was obtained (under the previous Section 14 of the Companies Act 1980) at the Extraordinary General Meeting on 25 October 1984 relates to the present total unissued share capital and will expire on 25 October 1989. In order to vest authority in the directors to allot shares not allocated to the capitalisation issue and employee share option schemes, an Ordinary Resolution in terms of Resolution 1(b) is required. Such authority, subject to earlier renewal or extension, will last for five years.

Moreover, the allotment of shares for cash, other than following a pro rata offer to existing shareholders, is prohibited by Section 89 of the Companies Act 1985 unless the shareholders first otherwise agree. At the last Annual General Meeting the authority was renewed for your directors to issue a limited number of Ordinary shares without first offering them to existing shareholders. This authority is limited to 1,900,000 Ordinary shares (5% of the authorised Ordinary share capital) and in Resolution 3, (which will be proposed as a Special Resolution), your directors propose the existing authority be revoked and fresh authority be granted over 3,300,000 Ordinary shares (5% of the enlarged authorised Ordinary share capital). The authority will, if granted and unless previously renewed, expire at the conclusion of the Company's Twenty First Annual General Meeting.

Extraordinary General Meeting.
The Extraordinary General Meeting to consider the relevant resolutions will be held on 3 October 1986. Notice of the Meeting appears on pages 6 and 7.

Action to be taken.
A Form of Proxy for the use of Ordinary shareholders at the Extraordinary General Meeting is enclosed. You are asked to complete and return the form in accordance with the instructions printed thereon as soon as possible but in any event so as to arrive at the Company's Registrars, National Westminster Bank PLC, not later than 2.30pm on Wednesday 1 October 1986. Completing and returning a form of proxy will not preclude you from attending the meeting and voting in person should you wish to do so. Please complete and return the form whether or not you propose to attend the meeting.

Your directors unanimously recommend you to vote in favour of the resolutions as they intend to do in respect of their beneficial holdings which amount to 1,894,503 Ordinary shares in British Vita PLC, representing approximately 6.25% of the issued Ordinary share capital.

Yours sincerely,

F. A. Carter

8 September 1986   Chairman

5

Notice is hereby given that an Extraordinary General Meeting of the Company will be held at the Registered Office of the Company, Soudan Street, Middleton, Manchester M24 2DB on Friday 3 October 1986 at 2.30pm for the purpose of considering and, if thought fit, passing the following Resolutions, the first two of which will be proposed as Ordinary Resolutions and the third as a Special Resolution.

Ordinary Resolutions

1 (a) That the authorised share capital of the Company be increased from £9,560,000 to £16,560,000 by the creation of 28,000,000 Ordinary shares of 25p each to rank *pari passu* in all respects with the existing issued 38,000,000 Ordinary shares in the capital of the Company.

1 (b) That the directors be and they are unconditionally authorised for the purpose of Section 80 of the Companies Act 1985 to allot relevant securities (as defined in that Act) up to an amount equal to the total unissued share capital in existence following the passing of the foregoing Resolution to such persons at such times and upon such terms and conditions as they may determine subject to the Company's Articles of Association provided that this authority shall, unless renewed, expire on the day of the fifth aniversary of the passing of this Resolution save that the Company may before such expiry make an offer or agreement which would or might require relevant securities to be allotted after such expiry and the Board may then allot relevant securities in pursuance of such offer or agreement as if the authority conferred hereby had not expired.

2 That subject to Resolution 1 being passed and upon the recommendation of the directors, the sum of £3,790,229.25, or other the sum required to give effect to this Resolution, being part of the amount now standing to the credit of the Company's share premium account be capitalised and the directors be authorised to appropriate such sum to the holders of Ordinary shares on the Register at the close of business on 26 September 1986 on the basis that such sum be applied in paying up at par 15,160,917, or other the number of shares required to give effect to this Resolution, new Ordinary shares of 25p each in the capital of the Company and to allot and issue the same, credited as fully paid up, to and amongst such members in the proportion of one Ordinary share of 25p each for every two existing Ordinary shares then held; such new Ordinary shares not to rank for the interim dividend to be paid on 10 November 1986 to Ordinary shareholders on the register on 3 October 1986 but otherwise to rank *pari passu* in all respects with the existing Ordinary shares in issue provided that no fraction of a share be so allotted but all such fractions be aggregated and allotted to a nominee to be appointed by the directors and sold for the benefit of the Company.

6

Special Resolution

3 That subject to Resolution 1 being passed the authority conferred on the directors under the Companies Act 1985 ("the Act") by the special resolution passed at the Twentieth Annual General Meeting of the Company be revoked and that in accordance with Section 95 of the Act and in substitution of the authority contained in Article 8 of the Company's Articles of Association, the directors be and they are hereby empowered to allot equity securities for cash (within the meaning of Section 94 of the Act) as if sub-section (i) of Section 89 of the Act did not apply to any such allotment and the directors may at any time prior to the expiry of the power hereby conferred, or any renewal thereof, make any offer or agreement which would or might require equity securities to be allotted after such expiry and the directors may allot equity securities in pursuance of such offer or agreement accordingly provided that the power hereby granted shall unless renewed expire at the conclusion of the Twenty First Annual General Meeting of the Company and shall be limited:

(i) to the allotment of equity securities in connection with a rights issue where it is reasonably necessary to allot equity securities otherwise than in accordance with Section 89 (i) of the Act; and

(ii) to the allotment (otherwise than pursuant to paragraph (i) above) of equity securities up to an aggregate nominal amount of £825,000.

By order of the Board
A.R. Teague
Secretary

Soudan Street,
Middleton,
Manchester
M24 2DB.

8 September 1986

Notes:

1. An Ordinary shareholder entitled to attend and vote is entitled to appoint one or more proxies (whether members or not) to attend and, on a poll, vote instead of him. A form of proxy must reach the Company's Registrars, National Westminster Bank PLC by 2.30pm on Wednesday 1 October 1986. A form of proxy is included for the use of Ordinary shareholders.

2. Subject to the passing of Resolutions 1 and 2 above, renounceable certificates for the new Ordinary shares arising from the capitalisation issue will be posted on 10 October 1986 to all holders registered at the close of business on 26 September 1986.

7

Index

(Note: Appendixes B, C and D have not been indexed.)

FOR THE BEST IN PAPERBACKS, LOOK FOR THE

In every corner of the world, on every subject under the sun, Penguin represents quality and variety – the very best in publishing today.

For complete information about books available from Penguin – including Pelicans, Puffins, Peregrines and Penguin Classics – and how to order them, write to us at the appropriate address below. Please note that for copyright reasons the selection of books varies from country to country.

In the United Kingdom: For a complete list of books available from Penguin in the U.K., please write to *Dept E.P., Penguin Books Ltd, Harmondsworth, Middlesex, UB7 0DA*

In the United States: For a complete list of books available from Penguin in the U.S., please write to *Dept BA, Penguin, 299 Murray Hill Parkway, East Rutherford, New Jersey 07073*

In Canada: For a complete list of books available from Penguin in Canada, please write to *Penguin Books Canada Ltd, 2801 John Street, Markham, Ontario L3R 1B4*

In Australia: For a complete list of books available from Penguin in Australia, please write to the *Marketing Department, Penguin Books Australia Ltd, P.O. Box 257, Ringwood, Victoria 3134*

In New Zealand: For a complete list of books available from Penguin in New Zealand, please write to the *Marketing Department, Penguin Books (NZ) Ltd, Private Bag, Takapuna, Auckland 9*

In India: For a complete list of books available from Penguin, please write to *Penguin Overseas Ltd, 706 Eros Apartments, 56 Nehru Place, New Delhi, 110019*

In Holland: For a complete list of books available from Penguin in Holland, please write to *Penguin Books Nederland B.V., Postbus 195, NL–1380AD Weesp, Netherlands*

In Germany: For a complete list of books available from Penguin, please write to *Penguin Books Ltd, Friedrichstrasse 10 – 12, D–6000 Frankfurt Main 1, Federal Republic of Germany*

In Spain: For a complete list of books available from Penguin in Spain, please write to *Longman Penguin España, Calle San Nicolas 15, E–28013 Madrid, Spain*

FOR THE BEST IN PAPERBACKS, LOOK FOR THE

A CHOICE OF PENGUINS AND PELICANS

A Question of Economics Peter Donaldson

Twenty key issues – the City, trade unions, 'free market forces' and many others – are presented clearly and fully in this major book based on a television series.

The Economist Economics Rupert Pennant-Rea and Clive Crook

Based on a series of 'briefs' published in the *Economist* in 1984, this important new book makes the key issues of contemporary economic thinking accessible to the general reader.

The Tyranny of the Status Quo Milton and Rose Friedman

Despite the rhetoric, big government has actually *grown* under Reagan and Thatcher. The Friedmans consider why this is – and what we can do now to change it.

Business Wargames Barrie G. James

Successful companies use military strategy to win. Barrie James shows how – and draws some vital lessons for today's manager.

Atlas of Management Thinking Edward de Bono

This fascinating book provides a vital repertoire of non-verbal images – to help activate the right side of any manager's brain.

The Winning Streak Walter Goldsmith and David Clutterbuck

A brilliant analysis of what Britain's best-run and successful companies have in common – a must for all managers.

A CHOICE OF PENGUINS AND PELICANS

Lateral Thinking for Management   Edward de Bono

Creativity and lateral thinking can work together for managers in developing new products or ideas; Edward de Bono shows how.

Understanding Organizations   Charles B. Handy

Of practical as well as theoretical interest, this book shows how general concepts can help solve specific organizational problems.

The Art of Japanese Management   Richard Tanner Pascale and Anthony G. Athos   With an Introduction by Sir Peter Parker

Japanese industrial success owes much to Japanese management techniques, which we in the West neglect at our peril. The lessons are set out in this important book.

My Years with General Motors   Alfred P. Sloan   With an Introduction by John Egan

A business classic by the man who took General Motors to the top – and kept them there for decades.

Introducing Management   Ken Elliott and Peter Lawrence (eds.)

An important and comprehensive collection of texts on modern management which draw some provocative conclusions.

English Culture and the Decline of the Industrial Spirit   Martin J. Wiener

A major analysis of why the 'world's first industrial nation has never been comfortable with industrialism'. 'Very persuasive' – Anthony Sampson in the *Observer*

A CHOICE OF PENGUINS AND PELICANS

Dinosaur and Co Tom Lloyd

A lively and optimistic survey of a new breed of businessmen who are breaking away from huge companies to form dynamic enterprises in microelectronics, biotechnology and other developing areas.

The Money Machine: How the City Works Philip Coggan

How are the big deals made? Which are the institutions that *really* matter? What causes the pound to rise or interest rates to fall? This book provides clear and concise answers to these and many other money-related questions.

Parkinson's Law C. Northcote Parkinson

'Work expands so as to fill the time available for its completion': that law underlies this 'extraordinarily funny and witty book' (Stephen Potter in the *Sunday Times*) which also makes some painfully serious points for those in business or the Civil Service.

Debt and Danger Harold Lever and Christopher Huhne

The international debt crisis was brought about by Western bankers in search of quick profit and is now one of our most pressing problems. This book looks at the background and shows what we must do to avoid disaster.

Lloyd's Bank Tax Guide 1987/8

Cut through the complexities! Work the system in *your* favour! Don't pay a penny more than you have to! Written for anyone who has to deal with personal tax, this up-to-date and concise new handbook includes all the important changes in this year's budget.

The Spirit of Enterprise George Gilder

A lucidly written and excitingly argued defence of capitalism and the role of the entrepreneur within it.

FOR THE BEST IN PAPERBACKS, LOOK FOR THE 🐧

PENGUIN DICTIONARIES

Archaeology
Architecture
Art and Artists
Biology
Botany
Building
Chemistry
Civil Engineering
Commerce
Computers
Decorative Arts
Design and Designers
Economics
English and European
   History
English Idioms
Geography
Geology
Historical Slang
Literary Terms
Mathematics

Microprocessors
Modern History 1789–1945
Modern Quotations
Physical Geography
Physics
Political Quotations
Politics
Proverbs
Psychology
Quotations
Religions
Saints
Science
Sociology
Surnames
Telecommunications
The Theatre
Troublesome Words
Twentieth Century History

FOR THE BEST IN PAPERBACKS, LOOK FOR THE

PENGUIN BUSINESS

Great management classics of the world (with brand new Introductions by leading contemporary figures); widely studied business textbooks; and exciting new business titles covering all the major areas of interest for today's businessman and businesswoman.

Parkinson's Law or **The Pursuit of Progress** C. Northcote Parkinson
My Years with General Motors Alfred P. Sloan Jr
Self-Help Samuel Smiles
The Spirit of Enterprise George Gilder
Dinosaur & Co: Studies in Corporate Evolution Tom Lloyd
Understanding Organizations Charles B. Handy
The Art of Japanese Management Richard Tanner Pascale & Anthony G. Athos
Modern Management Methods Ernest Dale & L. C. Michelon
Lateral Thinking for Management Edward de Bono
The Winning Streak Workout Book Walter Goldsmith & David Clutterbuck
The Social Psychology of Industry J. A. C. Brown
Offensive Marketing J. H. Davidson
The Anatomy of Decisions Peter G. Moore & H. Thomas
The Human Side of Enterprise Douglas McGregor
Corporate Recovery Stuart Slatter